EMYL JENKINS'

Pleasures of the Garden

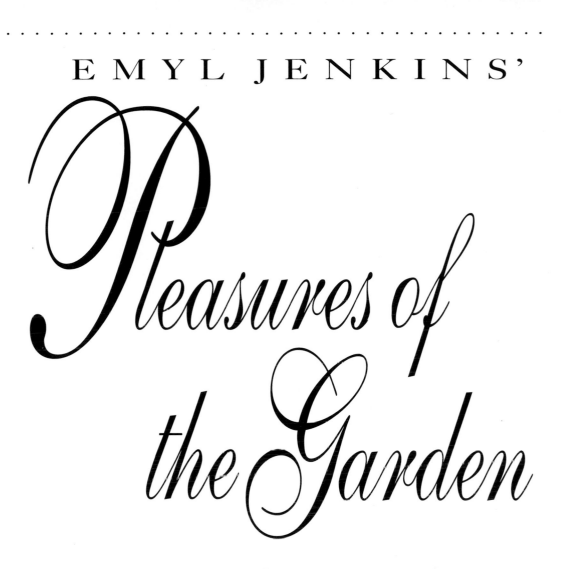

EMYL JENKINS'

Pleasures of the Garden

PHOTOGRAPHS BY

CHIP HENDERSON

AND EMYL JENKINS

~

FOREWORD BY

C.Z. GUEST

Crown Publishers, Inc.   New York

Books by Emyl Jenkins

⌒

Emyl Jenkins' Appraisal Book

*Emyl Jenkins' Guide to Buying and Collecting
Early American Furniture*

Emyl Jenkins' Southern Christmas

"Shears" by Robinson Jeffers (p. 111) is reprinted with the permission of Random House, Inc.
Lines from "Down the Garden Path" by Beverly Nichols (p.117) are used with the permission
of Doubleday, a division of Bantam Doubleday Dell Publishing Group, Inc.
Portions of "A Winter Garden's Secret" and "Family Gardens"
appeared previously in *Victoria* magazine.
In some cases where poems or verses are not acknowledged, the author has searched
diligently to find sources and to get permission to use them—but without success.

Published by Crown Publishers, Inc., 201 East 50th Street,
New York, New York 10022. Member of the Crown Publishing Group.
Random House, Inc. New York, Toronto, London, Sydney, Auckland
CROWN is a trademark of Crown Publishers, Inc.

Manufactured in Japan

Library of Congress Cataloging-in-Publication Data
Jenkins, Emyl.
[pleasures of the garden]
Emyl Jenkins' pleasures of the garden / Emyl Jenkins ;
photographs by Chip Henderson.—1st ed.
p.   cm.
Includes index.
1. Garden ornaments and furniture. 2. Gardens. 3. Gardens—Poetry. 4. Garden ornaments
and furniture—Pictorial works. 5. Gardens—Pictorial works. 6. Flower arrangement.
7. Flower arrangement—Pictorial works. I. Henderson, Chip. II. Title. 717—dc20
92-18788
CIP

ISBN 0-517-58525-1

10 9 8 7 6 5 4 3 2 1

FIRST EDITION

For
my father, Langdon Joslin,
my high school English teacher,
Granville Smith,
and my lifelong friend,
Mary Jane Bryant

CONTENTS

FOREWORD

hat a lovely book! *Pleasures of the Garden* by Emyl Jenkins. Any of us who has loved flowers for a lifetime can close our eyes and remember favorite fragrances, colors, bouquets, and the joys we've had putting them together.

   Pleasures of the Garden is a wonderful collection of personal gardening memories from Emyl Jenkins that are touching, often informative, funny at times, and quite inspirational. As I read her vignettes, I know that Emyl and I are soul mates. She still gets the same great pleasure from her garden as I have always gotten from mine.

If I were to close my eyes right now and think of a favorite gardening memory, my mind would wander back to more than thirty years ago. Another soul mate, one of my best friends, and the godfather to my two children, H.R.H. Duke of Windsor and I used to spend many an hour talking about our flowers, choosing plants and wandering around the glorious gardens of the Moulin de Tuileries outside of Paris. His favorite flower was the rose, and he had a vast rose garden that was to die for. He had every color imaginable and it was because of him that my garden was the first in America to have the beautiful orange tea rose Duke of Windsor imported from England. Oh! Those were the days of wine and roses!!!

As Emyl said in her book and I will repeat now, "to everything there is a season."

Times change, people come and go, but my garden is always there, a true and loyal friend. It always gives back to me the love and tenderness I put into it.

Good luck to Emyl with this joyous new book.

Happy Gardening,
C. Z. Guest
Summer of 1993

*"Everything is made
out of Magic, leaves and
trees, flowers and birds,
badgers and foxes and
squirrels and people.
So it must be all around
us. In this garden—
in all the places.
The Magic in this garden
has made me stand up
and know I am going
to live to be a man....
Every morning
and evening and
as often in the daytime
as I can remember
I am going to say,
'Magic is in me!'"*

~

The Secret Garden,
Frances Hodgson Burnett

INTRODUCTION:
GARDEN
MAGIC

*J*s there anyone who does not love a garden? Its beauty, its fragrance, its quietness, its glory, its little surprises, its magic?

Magic is everywhere in the garden. Yet ask the simple question, "What gives a garden its magic?" and each reply is as different as the person who is speaking.

"It is the flowers full blown," I was told in the lush months of May and June, everyone's favorite months.

*F*ew pleasures can compare to those we feel when we pause to drink in the beauty we find in the gardens that friends and strangers alike have provided for our enjoyment and enrichment.

*"Who loves
a garden
Finds
within
his soul
Life's
whole…"*

~

Louise
Seymour
Jones

Little surprises, dazzling colors, light and shadow, an infinite variety of textures, flawless beauty...

"It is the sun's golden glow filtering through autumn's radiant colors," the fall tourist in New England replied, camera in hand.

"It is the playful squirrels and singing birds that bring the promise of springtime before the trees bud out," an old gentleman told me with a twinkle in his eyes.

"It is the gates and the pathways—they seduce me," the sophisticated woman said in hushed tones.

"It is the little seeds," the pigtailed little girl giggled.

"It is the textures—the velvet leaves of the lamb's ear, the spiky thorns of the holly boughs, the satiny petals of the budding rose, the wiry curls of the bachelor's buttons," the learned scientist explained.

"It is the wind that, unseen, caresses the trees," the young poet rhapsodized.

"It is the hard work," my neighbor said, wiping the sweat from his brow as he looked around his garden, admiring his long day's labor.

"It is the colors—the soft rainbow colors and the brilliant display of fireworks that lasts for days in the garden instead of just a few moments in the sky," the romantic young girl breathlessly replied.

"It is a garden's hiding places," the overworked executive wistfully sighed.

"It is evidence on earth of God's generosity and handiwork," the clergyman extolled.

"It is the intimacy," the young lovers whispered in unison.

"It is the light and the shadow," the artist said, pausing to wait for the sun to come out from behind the clouds.

"It is the way the garden is designed," the landscape architect informed me.

"It is the statuary," the well-to-do couple exclaimed, their smiles and happy voices much friendlier than their outwardly formidable appearance suggested.

...these are visions to store away for a rainy day.

*Come,
the garden
beckons to
us. Now is
the time for
memories,
to reflect...
and to
dream.*

"It is the gardener," replied the garden curator, not surprisingly.

"It is . . . it is, the *magic*," said the well-seasoned garden lover.

Yes, there is magic everywhere in the garden. But its true magic is in the eye of the beholder, for garden magic is inside you.

Come with me now, through the garden gate, along winding pathways, to the old stone bench at the end of the green, down country roads, to the grand formal gardens of another time, on a walk through my neighborhood, to the nursery and the farmer's market, out to the seashore and up to the mountains, to behold gardens simple and majestic, quiet and exuberant, and find the magic.

~

"To know someone here or there with whom you can feel there is understanding in spite of distances or thoughts unexpressed—that can make of this earth a garden."

Goethe

"Where you tend a rose, my lad,

A thistle cannot grow."

The Secret Garden,

Frances Hodgson Burnett

MY GARDEN

My garden is my comfort, a sacred place where my spirit is restored, my mind refreshed, and my body rejuvenated.

Not everyone feels that way. Some of my friends tell me their gardens are a challenge. To them a garden is a place to be conquered, a wilderness to cultivate.

I tell them my garden is soothing. It is a sanctuary in the fullest meaning of the word.

*I*n October nature's purples and yellows become soothing and mellow, quite unlike spring's pastel hues and summer's bright splashes of color (below and opposite).

They say their gardens are time-consuming.

How can any moment spent in a garden be wasted time? I want to reply, but I think better of it. Instead, I turn my thoughts to my cherished moments in the garden, though, I admit, many of these are stolen moments, unseen by others and known only to me.

How I relish those quiet mornings when I can start the day by glancing out of my upstairs bedroom window to my garden below. Even in my groggy state I marvel at the orderly scheme of life I see there—an order that becomes more important to me with each passing year.

Year round, on sunny days and gray, an endless parade of wide-awake squirrels shimmy out to the farthest tips of the tangled oak branches. Recklessly they leap through the air. Intuitively they clutch the trunk of the nearby maple tree. Playfully they chase each other around and around until they reach the waiting ground. Still sleepy, I smile as I watch them scamper out of sight.

During the warm months of the year my early-morning sleep-heavy eyes feast upon a cheerful pageant of beauty and color in my flower bed. During the winter months, when the sight is more peaceful than uplifting, I find comfort in

knowing that the next generation of those very same flowers are waiting patiently for the warm sun to draw near before they send up tender shoots. In no time at all, those little plants will grow and blossom before my very eyes.

And in every season the birds sing.

No matter how leisurely the morning begins, the day that follows is always too short. There are untold phone calls, unfinished tasks, unanticipated interruptions, unessential worries, and unexpected kindnesses.

Quite often these days people ask me, "How do you do so much? Don't the pressures get to you?"

Of course they do, but I have found the world is much less stressful because in the back of my mind I hold dear my early-morning view of my garden. It stays with me through the day. It helps to keep the day, and life, in perspective.

In the late afternoon, once again I steal a moment. As I look out over my garden from the downstairs kitchen window that faces west, I watch the red sunset mark the end of daylight hours. Only moments later I gaze in equal wonderment as twilight's fire-red sky turns a rich cobalt blue sprinkled with a million glistening stars and a solitary moon.

Day by day, I find solace in the familiar, constant, and comfortable patterns ever present in my garden. Over the years I have come to realize that my moods follow my garden's colors season by season.

In fall's contemplative gold and purple garden I relive dreamy images of my

now-past youth and ponder what lies ahead. In spring's tender green and blush-pink garden I cast those times aside and I anticipate happy times yet ahead. In summer's dazzling red and yellow garden I am restless and fitful. I am anxious for a cooler, quieter time. In winter's

"There is a pleasure in the pathless wood, There is a rapture on the lonely shore . . ."
~
Lord Byron

peaceful, resting garden I reach inside myself and seek inner peace. Each season has its own place as time rolls forward and we approach a new millennium.

At any given time, when I think forward or backward to an upcoming or a bygone season, I remember only the best of my garden—the maple leaves that turned just the right color of gold, the snowdrops that waited until the snow finally did come in March before dying down, and the amaryllis I brought inside in October that took off like a shooting star the day after Christmas and bloomed for Valentine's Day. I never dwell upon the fifty anemone bulbs that didn't come up, the asters that wilted and rotted off at the ground, or the week it didn't rain when I was away and there was no one to water the flower beds. How I wish my garden were filled only with beauty! But this cannot be.

Every year Japanese beetles bore

nail-like holes in my most-prized yellow roses, leaving untouched the dark red ones I'm not that fond of. Ice storms and freezing temperatures viciously attack the ever-vulnerable Pink Perfection camellia shrubs, turning the outer tips of their pale pink blossoms a scorched, ugly brown. The same night graceful azalea shrub boughs that grace my front door are randomly snapped off. But unsightly dead limbs way too high for me to prune escape unscathed.

And the March wind never fails to whip through the wobbly limbs of the young willow tree where an eager family of birds unwisely built its nest. The next morning I find their fragile, cuplike straw and twig home on the ground. These unfortunate, and unpreventable, occurrences do not mean my garden is a morose or a sad place. It is anything but.

Cheerful little surprises are everywhere in every season. In late January a lone, frilly petaled pink oxalis sheltered by broad, cloverlike leaves blooms its little heart out. In mid-June one dwarf iris, too timid to bloom along with the others in May, unfurls its lacy white petals. And in September the prettiest daisylike chrysanthemum you've ever seen appears in the most unlikely and inappropriate of places—in the middle of my rose garden!

I see nature's manifold and various wonders in my garden any time of the year. As I wander alone, I delight in life's joys and forgive life's pettiness.

How much more content all of our lives would be if we spent more time in

our gardens—especially those times when our burdens are the heaviest and we become self-absorbed.

In the garden we mortals can find life's deeper meaning and behold life's scheme. In the garden, as we look around us, we begin to understand how it all fits together. In bustling gardens we see the dark and ugly living side by side with things that are bright and beautiful. In quiet twilight gardens we touch an intimacy within ourselves. And always, if only we look for it, we can glimpse moments of humor and light. But most important, in the privacy of the garden you can nurture your soul, your vision of the world. You see, when you fall under the magical spell of the garden you can find inner peace.

In my garden I see, I observe, I think, and I resolve. I do these things because I do not preach, nor do I write poetry. But I do pray the gardener's prayer.

Help us, O Lord, to grasp the meaning of growing things, and the mystery of opening bud, that we may weave it into our faith and life eternal.

Give us wisdom to cultivate our minds as diligently as we nurture tender seedlings and patience to weed out envy and malice as we uproot weeds.

Teach us to seek steady root growth rather than a fleeting culture, and to cultivate the things which brighten under adversity with perennial loveliness.

Thank God for gardens.

And, I would add, for the comfort they provide.

The glorious magic of a late winter sunset creates a fiery nature garden.

In the South the petticoat-ruffled pink petals of the Pink Perfection (opposite) promise perfect spring days to come.

$\mathcal{G}$arden Magic is all around you . . . from breathtaking vistas like Thomas Jefferson's from his mountaintop home, Monticello, in Charlottesville, Virginia (opposite), to carefully orchestrated gardens at Orton Plantation in Wilmington, North Carolina (opposite below), to the lush borders that line the walkways of The Barnyard in Carmel, California (right).

A Gift from the Garden
AMARYLLIS

Novice gardeners should remember that prepotted amaryllis bulbs are almost foolproof. For Christmas blooms, begin your bulbs when available.

Most amaryllis, whether bought loose or prepotted, have simple instructions attached. But understanding a flower's preferences starts your "growing" relationship off to a better start. So here are a few tips.

Though the amaryllis bulb is large, its pot should be small; a 4- or 5-inch diameter pot is ample for the average-size bulb. Amaryllis bulbs like their roots "bound" and respond to this crowded treatment by sending up bigger flowers.

If you buy a loose bulb and pot it in a new clay pot, first thoroughly soak the pot. On the bottom of the pot put a half-inch layer of marbles or gravel. This provides good drainage and keeps the soil from clotting. Fill the pot half full of rich potting soil mixed with a handful of bone meal. Gently press the bulb down so the roots spread out into the soil. When the roots are well covered by the dirt, pack additional soil around the bulb until it is two-thirds covered up. Firmly press the soil around the bulb so there are no air bubbles. Leave the top third portion of the bulb uncovered.

Water thoroughly and place in a warm, sunny spot. A bright southern exposure window near a heat vent is ideal. (My father begins his amaryllis bulbs on top of the clothes dryer, which sits beneath a window that gets the afternoon sun.) Peep in on the bulb every couple of days. Keep the soil damp, but not wet. When the flower stalk begins to shoot up increase your watering, now keeping the soil very moist. (Part of the fun of growing an amaryllis is watching its visible, Jack-and-the-beanstalk growth.) If you began the bulb in an out-of-the-way place, move it out for all to admire when the first flower head begins to open.

To keep the weighty flower head from becoming top-heavy, sink an attractive stake deep in the soil and secure the stalk to it with a twist-tie. (If the plant should topple over, amaryllis blossoms can also be cut and used as long-lasting cut flowers.) It is now best to keep the plant in a cooler but bright spot, so the flowers will last as long as possible.

As each individual blossom fades, snip it off. When the last bloom wilts, cut off the entire flower stalk. (Many bulbs will send up a second flower stalk. If so, treat it the same way as the first flowers and stalk.)

You now have a bulb with lovely foliage that will continue to be green and attractive and put out new leaves, but no new flowers, through the summer and early fall months. You can keep the bulb in its pot and sink it into the ground, or place it on a patio during these warm months. Do not cut any of the leaves. The leaf growth feeds the bulb for the next season. Continue to water and lightly fertilize the bulb until the first of October. If an early frost is expected, bring the pot inside.

Discontinue watering. When the leaves have wilted, cut them off and place the pot on its side and keep it in a warm place. After three to four weeks of "resting" (around November first), put the pot in a slightly cooler but dry spot and leave it there until early December. Now bring the bulb out. If a larger pot is needed repot the bulb with fresh soil and begin the bulb's life anew. The bulb will flower for years, its flowers becoming larger and more plentiful as it ages.

*M*any
nineteenth-
century garden-
ers considered
dahlias gaudy.
They preferred
more fragile
flowers—prim-
roses, lily-of-the-
valley, roses.
Today we delight
in the dahlia's
exotic, bold
colors, alluring
shapes and
textures, and
their long-lasting
blooms.

In God's great out-of-doors every season, every place has its own charm, its unique beauty, its indescribable magic. I love them all.

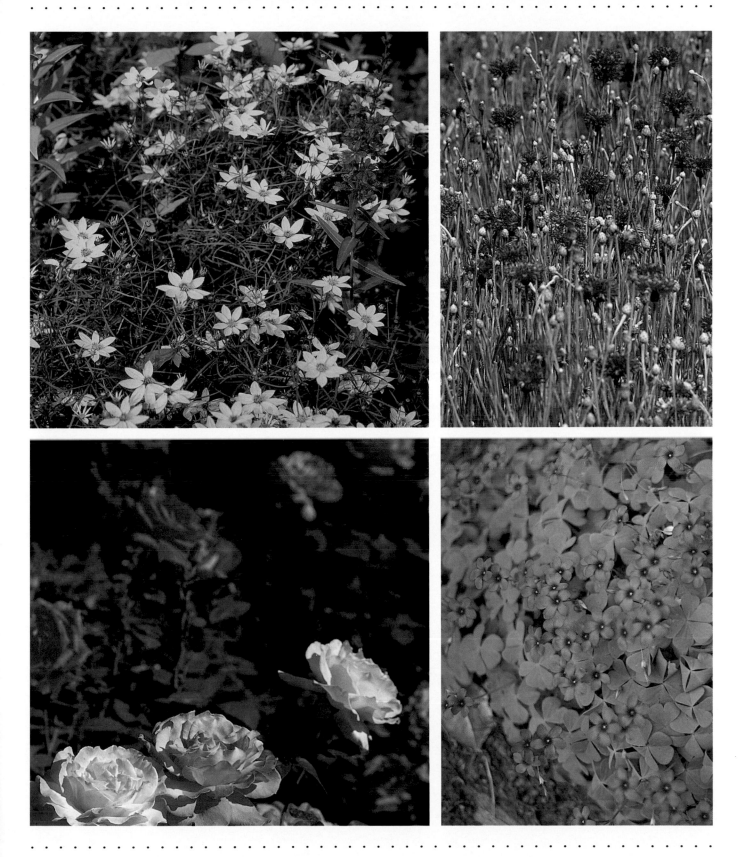

"Heard melodies are sweet,

but those unheard are sweeter."

"Ode on a Grecian Urn," John Keats

A WINTER GARDEN'S SECRET

*J*love my wintertime garden. Looking across the frost-tipped lawn that stretches out to the street in front and the driveway in back, some people would ask, What garden? They think there must be flowers for the earth to deserve the title "garden." Not I. My winter garden has a stalwart beauty all its own.

Already this year, like last, its tall, stately trees, veterans of so many winters, have quietly bent under relentless winds and

A winter garden has a beauty all its own. On somber, gray days we pause to admire the deep blanket of ivy and the gnarled and tangled limbs of the bittersweet shrub that catch our eye.

*N*o winter colors are more beautiful than those of snow-white camellia blossoms (left) surrounded by deep, waxy green leaves.

heavy ice. Two killing frosts have nipped the restless camellia blooms that tried to rush the season. Yet miraculously they, and the waxy green boxwood shrubs that shelter my front door, still grow and prosper without pampering or coaxing.

I can't say the same for my summer-

for now I find beauty in the stillness of my always-there winter garden. And in those short days of winter, when the sun casts long, deep shadows so early in the afternoon, and the blue of night rushes in quickly after the sun sets, I find the familiar beauty of the winter garden to

time garden. As soon as the frost passes, an endless round of garden tasks begins. First the ground must be prepared. Next new seeds must be sown and green-house-nurtured plants set into the ground. Later I will have to water and fertilize, pinch back spindly blossoms, and train unruly stalks around trellises.

But those tasks are for another time;

be as restorative as a cup of hot tea.

During the spring and summer months so much needs to be done in the garden it is easy to feel frustrated from the outset. Clusters of lilies-of-the-valley given to me by my dear friend Pickett Guthrie from her mother's garden must be painstakingly divided so each delicate flower will have its own, uncrowded

When the star-shaped blossoms of summer's pink and blue hydrangeas change to winter beige, they resemble mounds of snowflakes frozen to last the season.

"Lowly, sprightly little flower! Herald of a brighter bloom, Bursting in a sunny hour From thy winter tomb!"

"To the Crocus," Mrs. Patterson

space. And if I don't take the time to properly feed the elegant yellow-bearded irises they won't be half so regal next year. Like my children when they were small, my flowers demand my total attention at this most-busy time of year.

Not so with my dormant winter garden. It seems perfectly content in its quietness. So I remind myself it would be pointless to take on garden tasks in the dead of winter. Anyway, I'm happy to have a rest from digging and toiling. Like my garden, I too am content in my quietness. How nice it is to have a little thinking time.

One year, when an impassable snowstorm kept me housebound, as I gazed out over the colorless sprawling lawn I asked myself, What makes the sparse winter garden so special? In my solitude I found the answer: It is the silence.

My winter garden has, like Keats's unheard sweet melodies, a silent beauty unseen by human eyes. A January garden is imbued with the same voiceless charm as the ornamental stone figures that endure all seasons in my garden. And like those statues, the wintertime garden harbors many ageless secrets.

Hidden beneath the crusty earth, wiry roots of spring-blooming bulbs are growing strong under the thick blanket of brown leaves dropped by the century-old trees that line my yard. High in those same trees there are secret hollows where bushy-tailed squirrels, toasty warm in their gray winter coats, dine on their private store of acorns and hickory nuts.

And the clouds that hover overhead hold yet other secrets. Oh, on tonight's newscast the meteorologist may tell me that snow is on the way, or that tomorrow will be a clear but crisp sunny day—but I know I must wait until dawn to find out what the day really will bring.

It doesn't matter that I can't see the green tips of the crocuses hidden by the dried leaves, or peep into the squirrels' secret nest, or know what the clouds hold—I still love my winter garden.

Only in winter do we see the stark, enduring beauty that the lush spring, summer, and fall months will soon be-mask. When the earth is still and bare, the somber gray-brown bark of a hickory tree trunk is quite satisfying in itself. Then, more than at any other time, I enjoy the deep hunter green ivy that cascades over the aged brick wall beside my kitchen door. Later, when cheerful pink and white impatiens bloom in the shadows cast by the fully leafed limbs of the hickory tree, and the purple clematis bursts into full blossom among the ivy, spring's marvels will divert my eye.

But winter's colors can be breathtaking. In that brief, fleeting moment at sunset when the orange sky becomes a canvas for a maze of twisted, intertwined black tree limbs, I pause—and I thrill at the sight.

True, sunsets linger longer in the spring. How I look forward to twilight's springtime burst of color! Those first warm days of April, when spring with its inescapable daylight saving time arrives, I feel compelled to stay outside until the last ray of light fades. Somehow, though, in my rush to finish one more task before the sun goes down, I invariably miss seeing the sunset. And even in summer's stifling-hot temperatures I tough out the day and go inside only when I can no longer see to weed the stray stalks of wire grass that sprouted in between the black-eyed Susans and blackberry lilies. Hours later I will wonder, When did it get dark?

But in winter's silence, I take the time to savor the last light of the fading sun. Then, as night's darkness looms, I turn away before the sky becomes pitch-black. I am content. Life is unhurried in the glow of my warm home which is as comfortable and snug as the sleeping squirrels' lair.

In my wintertime garden, no butterflies flutter, no honeybees hum. There are no whimsical Johnny-jump-up faces or graceful summer dahlias. Yet I know each is safely hidden away in its own secret bed where winter's silence holds the promise of spring's exuberance.

Through the years I have learned that to every thing there *is* a season. Later will be the time to plant and to pluck that which was planted. Now is the season to keep the secrets. Now is the time to relish the silence.

~

"Like a dear old lady
Dressed in soft brown cashmere
Sitting with quiet, folded hands,
content and peaceful
And smiling a mysterious promise,
My winter garden waits."

"A Portrait,"
Caroline Giltiana

A *Gift from the Garden*
DRIED ARRANGEMENTS

Dried arrangements are most attractive during the late fall and winter months, especially if you are in a woodsy mood when the air is as crisp as the dry leaf's rustle. A walk along a stream or pond or around a country field can yield wonderful natural grasses and foliage.

It takes a lot of imagination to create a lovely piece out of little more than grass and straw and a twisted branch. But you can easily make whimsical "everlasting" arrangements like these made by Huntley Friend of Chatham, Virginia.

Take a thick handful of sun-dried wheat and wrap and tie it with straw to create a stunning arrangement in a spatter-painted terra-cotta flowerpot (bottom). To hold it in place, position the stems in the center of the flowerpot. Pour quick-drying plaster of paris around it, filling the pot about three-quarters full. When this composition dries, cover it with a little Spanish moss, sheet moss, or even pebbles.

To make the arrangement at top, use a single branch with a naturally bent "arm." This limb is held secure in its container by plaster of paris. Glue a store-bought bird's nest basket filled with a snug-fitting piece of Styrofoam on the branch. Stick into the foam any variety of interesting dried grasses, straws, rosehips, chinaberry balls, even small cattails, crepe myrtle spires, or cotton bolls for contrast.

A Gift from the Garden

HERB, FRUIT, AND
FLOWER GARLANDS

*I*n wintertime a cheerful garland of herbs and fruits can brighten any room in the house. A string of bay leaves, nutmeg, cinnamon sticks, dried fruits, and dwarf Indian corn ears tied with red and white gingham fits snugly on the open door of my nineteenth-century pine corner cupboard in the guest bedroom. The combination of rich fragrances and warm earth colors of the dormant winter garden adds a lovely seasonal touch to the indoors.

Nothing could be simpler to make. Gather together the herbs listed above, as well as any other dried herbs or even flowers or foliage that strike your fancy. To prepare the dried fruit (though of course you can buy them already dried), thinly slice apples and oranges crosswise, removing the core and seeds. Spread out the slices evenly on a sheet of pierced (prick with a fork) aluminum foil. Place in a 180-degree oven until dry. Overnight is best. The slices are then ready to be strung. Arrange the material you have chosen in a pleasing way so the colors, shapes, and textures are mixed. String them together using a large needle and fishing line. Sew on appropriate ribbons or fabric at the ends to make an attractive bow for a dressier appearance, or use large loops for an informal setting.

_I_n the olden days no house was without its beautiful and distinctive "ivy tree" (left), or the perennially green mistletoe tree (top), so indispensable at Christmastide when feuding neighbors and hopeful lovers alike found its charm irresistible.

$\mathcal{Q}$uiet drifting snow casts a magical spell across the garden—a beautiful scene of black and white seen no other time of the year (left).

$\mathcal{D}$on't you miss the snow?" my northern friends often ask me. Of course I do. But when the aptly named Star of Bethlehem blooms each spring, a beautiful snowlike blanket of blooms turns green lawns white and, like real snow, lasts only a few days, soon to be followed by a dusting of pink cherry blossoms (opposite).

SNOWDROP

*M*rs. Robinson, a nineteenth-century poet, wrote about the snow-drops, "Amidst the bare and chilling gloom, / A beauteous gem appears." Snowdrops, their bell-shaped white blossoms befitting their name, bloom long before the crocuses peep through the warm bed of leaves that warm the earth when the midwinter sun rises high in the sky and stays longer through the day.

*T*he deep rose color of the sky foreshadows the spring soon to come. But when spring arrives, it will not be the sky but the roses in our garden that will catch our eye. Then we will no longer see the wondrous intri-cacies of perfectly formed trees that remind us of a masterfully detailed pencil and charcoal drawing.

"Earth's crammed with Heaven,
And every common bush afire with God."

Elizabeth Barrett Browning

GREAT EXPECTATIONS

*S*pring truly did come in February this year. Overnight my backyard turned from an unkept lawn of dingy brown leaves into a meadow of wind-kissed yellow daffodils warmed by a thicket of star-shaped blue periwinkle. A week later the handful of curly-tipped clusters of fragrant paperwhite narcissus that had bloomed beneath the oak tree since December began to droop. And

*I*n a sheltered patch of earth made cozy by a layer of newly fallen oak leaves and the sun's warmth on the rocks, the first star-shaped periwinkle blooms announce spring is almost here (above).

*M*y grandmother would never have clustered purple, yellow, and red flowers together in her prim, Southern, ladylike, old-fashioned garden (right).

while I watched, a flock of robins grew plump in front of my eyes as they plucked the berries, one by one, from the burfordi holly at the corner of the house.

This year, like last year and the year before, some time in summer or fall I will wonder, just when did the periwinkle bloom? Did the robins come in January, or was it early February? Did I pick the first daffodils for Valentine's Day, or was it later? I'll wonder, shrug my own questions off, and resolve to be more precise in my observations next year.

How I admire my friends who keep a gardening calendar! How fascinating it is to hear them report that a certain variety of iris that bloomed on April Fools' Day two years ago did not open until April twelfth this year. These are my same friends who plot their gardens on graph paper. These are the ones who transplant, or discard completely, a too-purplish azalea bush that doesn't blend with the colors around it. These are my neighbors who plan ahead which plants they will buy and know exactly where they will plant them.

My ways are not their ways. I do not keep a calendar. I don't sketch my garden out on blue-lined paper. I buy plants and seeds impulsively, indiscriminately. Worse yet, I plant them that way.

I don't do it intentionally. Every spring I diligently scour through old and new garden-design books looking for the perfect scheme. I become obsessed with the task at hand. Far into the night I read and study.

"The best-looking gardens usually feature one dominant flower shape," I read in my newly organized frame of mind. "Mass plantings have more impact than the same amount scattered from place to place," I commit to memory. "Every line drawn on the plan must refer specifically to some real physical element on the ground," I pore over twice to make sure I have grasped the concept. "If one has greenhouse space there are many shrubs worth growing in pots, and bringing into bloom early for the house," I read, dreaming of the greenhouse space I wish I had.

Inspired, educated, edified, and well-intended, this year I stood ready to attack my garden and start anew. Other years I didn't have the same determination. This year, though, I knew I had to do something. My garden was a mess. All I had to do was think back to last summer to know this was the case. It was a hot July day when some unexpected visitors dropped by. "We'd love to see your garden," they said. I spent the rest of the afternoon apologizing for my riotous flowers' misbehavior.

The Johnny-jump-ups had taken over. They were supposed to have bloomed in March, but they had waited until April. Now there they were, in late summer, refusing to die, and I refused to yank them up. Meanwhile, the zinnias, the staple of a summer Southern garden, forgot to bloom.

"What are those?" one dear lady asked, gesturing in the air. "Those," I figured out, were the astilbes, all powder-

JOHNNY-JUMP-UP

Despite winter's lingering chill, sometimes as early as January a single Johnny-jump-up appears in my garden. Usually he jumps up beneath a protective rosemary plant in my herb garden. Snug beneath this warm blue cloak, and tempted by the lengthening January sun, Johnny jumps up bravely and mischievously, and blossoms forth.

Through the years, this cheerful little fellow has gathered more names than any other single flower. In fact, author Alice Earle called it "Ladies' Delight" rather than "Johnny-jump-up." Here, for *your* delight, is her passage about its early blooming, and its many enchanting names.

For several years the first blossom of the new year . . . was neither the Snowdrop nor Crocus, but the Ladies' Delight, that laughing, speaking little garden face, which is not really a spring flower, it is a stray from summer; but it is such a shrewd, intelligent little creature that it readily found out that spring was here ere man or other flowers knew it. . . . It has a score of folk names, all testifying to an affectionate intimacy: Bird's-eye, Garden gate; Johnny-jump-up; None-so-pretty; Kitty-come; Kit-run-about; Three-faces-under-a-hood; Come-and-cuddle-me; Pink-of-my-Joan; Kiss-me; Tickle-my-fancy; Kiss-me-ere-I-rise; Jump-up-and-kiss-me. To our little flower has also been given this folk name, Meet-her-in-the-entry-kiss-her-in-the-buttery, the longest plant name in the English language. . . . These little Ladies' Delights have infinite variety of expression; some are laughing and roguish, some sharp and shrewd, some surprised, others worried, all are animated and vivacious, and a few saucy to a degree. They are as companionable as people—nay, more; they are as companionable as children. No wonder children love them; they recognize kindred spirits!

puff pink, stately yet delicately airy, and absolutely irresistible in each and every catalog picture I had seen. But the plants she was pointing to were dingy brown, stumpy, and singularly unattractive in my garden.

"Well, your ageratum has done well," her friend exclaimed, when no one could

think of anything kind to say about the astilbes. Every spring, my friend Scotty Bowers tells me to avoid ageratum because it gets leggy and ragged and then turns sandy brown in the Southern heat. Last summer my ageratum border was lush, compact, and the prettiest shade of lilac purple I've ever seen.

"Oh, and I see you have marigolds," the first lady said sweetly. How could anyone not see I had marigolds, I thought

to myself. Unfortunately, someone had mislabeled the flat of twenty-four marigold plants I had bought. The blossoms I thought were going to be all frilly and pale yellow turned out to be boldly striped and Mexican orange.

Yes, this spring I will do better, I promised myself.

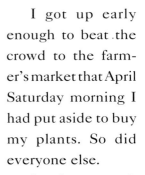

I got up early enough to beat the crowd to the farmer's market that April Saturday morning I had put aside to buy my plants. So did everyone else.

It takes a much stronger person than I am to resist the newest salmon pink geraniums with white scalloped trim outlining their petals, deep yellow coreopsis with orange button centers, and snow-white Boston daisies with their fernlike dark green leaves, to say nothing of the already blooming red, pink, yellow, and orange velvety snapdragons that beg to have their little faces pinched.

In no time at all, I surrendered my best intentions and went back to my old habits. I grabbed two of the empty boxes waiting at the end of each aisle and crammed as many plants as I could into them. Soon I was pointing out my additional choices to the helpful young clerk

How anyone can resist choosing at least one color of every flower is more than I'll ever know.

 kaleido-scope of textures and colors captured at noon in the midsummer Southern sun are as bright as any image of Joseph's coat.

Firecracker-red spider lilies literally shoot up overnight, their spidery blossoms at the top of a single green stalk. Like fireworks, their brilliance lasts only a short time—no more than a couple of weeks. Then their plain (by comparison) slender green leaves follow. But while they are in bloom they are unparalleled for show and splendor.

Brilliant, colorful zinnias are so common-place in the summer garden that most people take them for granted. But they are wonderfully varied. They come in almost every color imaginable, and if you take the time to look at them carefully, you will note cheerful little surprises among their blossoms. Who would expect a cluster of a hundred red eyes to peep out from these golden yellow petals (right) or the curled-up leaves of this crimson-red zinnia to wear a white petticoat beneath (above left)? This button-like variety (above right) was a favorite among the children's gardens at the turn of the century and was most aptly named "crested and crinkled" after its rolled-over petals that resemble the puffy skirts of olden days.

who offered to carry my new garden up to the cash register. Meanwhile I moved on to the hostas.

Isn't there a bare spot among the variegated hostas that line the shady spot on the western side of the house, I wondered. While trying to visualize last year's garden, I spied a new hosta, "Great Expectations." Its creamy center and forest-green border seemed quite unlike any of the many varieties I already had. Even if it were a perfect match for others in the garden, its name alone would have made it a have-to-have plant. *Great Expectations* was, and is, my favorite Dickens novel.

My arms once again full, this time with a clump of hosta, I was telling myself I had done enough damage for one day when a total stranger passed by carrying the most exquisite pale-blue delphinium plant I had ever seen outside of my New England grandmother's garden.

You know delphinium will not grow in the South, I reminded myself at the same time I asked him where he had found his. Following his directions I dashed over to snatch up the second-, third-, and fourth-best plants before anyone else could. "Mass plantings have more impact," I remembered, gathering up yet another tall spike. What does it matter in April that they will wither in our 90-plus-degree rainless July season?

Fighting my way through the ever-growing crowd back to the cash register I accidently brushed against the revolving seed-display rack. For years I have meant to try to coax along a stand of early spring

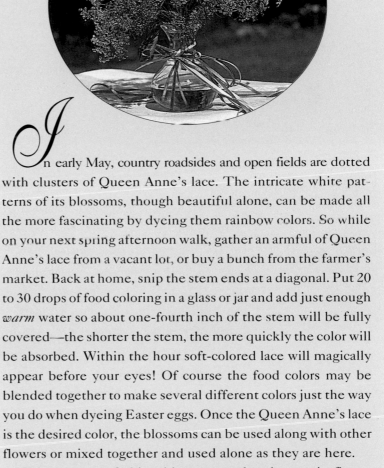

A Gift from the Garden
COLORED GARDEN LACE

In early May, country roadsides and open fields are dotted with clusters of Queen Anne's lace. The intricate white patterns of its blossoms, though beautiful alone, can be made all the more fascinating by dyeing them rainbow colors. So while on your next spring afternoon walk, gather an armful of Queen Anne's lace from a vacant lot, or buy a bunch from the farmer's market. Back at home, snip the stem ends at a diagonal. Put 20 to 30 drops of food coloring in a glass or jar and add just enough *warm* water so about one-fourth inch of the stem will be fully covered—the shorter the stem, the more quickly the color will be absorbed. Within the hour soft-colored lace will magically appear before your eyes! Of course the food colors may be blended together to make several different colors just the way you do when dyeing Easter eggs. Once the Queen Anne's lace is the desired color, the blossoms can be used along with other flowers or mixed together and used alone as they are here.

It is no longer fashionable to use colored water in flower arrangements, but I remember how in the 1940s and '50s ladies used to add just a few drops of food coloring when arranging flowers in clear containers. When dyeing flowers add only a little bit of water to your food coloring, otherwise the color will become too diluted. More water was added here so the colored water could be clearly seen.

*O*nce my bounty
of garden beau-
ties is home, the
fun—and the
challenge—of
deciding where
to put them
all begins.

consequences of my indulgences. There could be no rhyme or reason, much less a grand scheme to how all those plants, seeds, and bulbs could possibly be squeezed into the carefully delineated lines I had seen in the pages of *Landscape Architecture, Horticulture Today,* and *Better Homes & Gardens'* garden specials, to say nothing of the past three years' worth of *Southern Living* garden features I had meticulously clipped and filed away in manila folders for safekeeping.

And so I began setting my new plants out with great abandon. Where there had been a bald spot seconds before, a freshly packed-in flower suddenly appeared, ready for a long drink of water and a dousing of fertilizer for good measure. There was no place for three, much less five delphinium plants to be massed together.

While planting a particularly voluptuous ruffly lavender petunia next to an already established prim cone flower with stiff, pointed petals, I vaguely recalled the advice, "The best-looking gardens usually feature one dominant flower shape." Looking around, I couldn't find two flower shapes that even resembled each other! So much for that theory. I giggled as I resumed digging and planting, my heart as light as the butterfly that darted about, inspecting my work.

It was almost dark before I settled back on the fresh green lawn to muse upon how much fun I had had since early morning. Only then did I take the time to admire my once-again mismatched but oh, so bountiful garden.

sweet peas, but I never am in a seed store in January, the time they have to be sown. So what if it is too late again this year? Maybe if I buy them now and tack the package up on my bulletin board I'll remember to plant them *next* January, I rationalized. In my nicest way I asked the hapless lady who happened to be standing nearby to please put under my chin the envelope of seeds I was nodding toward.

By the time I had checked out, I had at least one variety of every plant I had even considered adding to my garden, whether seed, plant, or out-of-season and on-sale bulb. It would take a tractor to plough a tract large enough to hold my purchases, and my little plot was already overcrowded.

Once the pots, flats, and bags were out of the trunk, backseat, and passenger side of the car, I faced up to the

PLANNING
THE GARDEN
Amy Lowell

Bring pencils, fine pointed,
For our writing must be infinitesimal;
And bring sheets of paper
To spread before us.
Now draw the plan of our garden beds,
And outline the borders and the paths
Correctly.
We will scatter little words
Upon the paper,
Like seeds about to be planted;
We will fill all the whiteness
With little words,
So that the brown earth
Shall never show between our flowers;
Instead there will be petals and greenness
From April till November.

These narrow lines
Are rose-drifted thrift,
Edging the paths.
And here I plant nodding columbines,
With tree-tall wistarias behind them,
Each stem umbrella's in its purple fringe,
Winged sweet-peas shall flutter next to pansies
All down the sunny centre.

Foxglove spears,
Thrust back against the swaying lilac leaves,
Will bloom and fade before the China asters
Smear their crude colours over the Autumn hazes.
These double paths dividing make an angle
For bushes,
Bleeding-hearts, I think,
Their flowers jigging
Like little ladies,
Satined, hoop-skirted,
Ready for a ball.

The round black circles
Mean striped and flaunting tulips,
The clustered trumpets of yellow jonquils,
And the sharp blue of hyacinths and squills,
These specks like dotted grain
Are coreopsis, bright as bandanas,
And ice-blue heliotrope with its sticky leaves,
And mignonette
Whose sober-coloured cones of bloom
Scent quiet mornings.
And poppies! Poppies! Poppies!
The hatchings shall all mean a tide of poppies,
Crinkled and frail and flowing in the breeze.

Wait just a moment,
Here's an empty space.
Now plant me lilies of the valley—
This pear tree over them will keep them cool—
We'll have a lot of them
With white bells jingling.
The steps
Shall be all soft with stone-crop;
And at the top I'll make an arch of roses,
Crimson,
Bee-enticing.
There, it is done;
Seal up the paper.
Let us go to bed and dream of flowers.

"this is the garden: colours come and go . . . absolute lights like baths of golden snow."

~

e. e. cummings

You see, long ago I learned that the best garden of all is the garden that reflects life's multitude of choices. In all good intentions we mortals love to plan and plot, scheme and arrange. We delight in trying to compartmentalize our lives. But when you are offered a bounty of possible riches, a feast of promises that just might blossom forth, how can you pick and choose and knowingly select only the right ones? I certainly can't—especially when past experiences have taught me that even the most educated guess will be right only part of the time.

Like life, my garden is made up of chance encounters and subtle lessons. Neither I, nor you, nor any of our best-intended friends can know for sure just what will work year in and year out. This is why I fill my garden to overflowing with grand opportunities. I toil among my new crop of plants. I love and nurture them, hoping for the best, but always expecting the unexpected. In the end, I know there will be disappointments, but these will be offset by wonderful surprises.

Of course the delphinium won't make it past June—that's a given. Maybe this year the astilbes will do better, though. At least I bought marigolds that were already opening this time and I know they are yellow, not orange. And who knows how the new hosta will fare? Still, I have great expectations for it!

~

"Earth, I thank you for the pleasure of your language."

Anne Spencer

Since time immemorial a bountiful harvest has been one of God's greatest gifts to mankind. As far back as the second century A.D., the Roman poet Septimus Serenus exclaimed that a garden is a goodly thing, it ". . . charms, allures, gives shelter, food."

THE LANGUAGE OF FLOWERS

*T*he language of flowers is a romantic language, full of beauty and symbolism. Only love has been written about more frequently and more passionately than flowers. And how often the two are intertwined!

"The most charming of all gifts is one of flowers. A queen may give them to her subjects; and the poorest subject may

A rose for love, a daisy for hope, and ivy for marriage (above) say "I love you and I hope you will marry me."

*S*prays of forget-me-nots and sweet peas (above right) remind the receiver, "Do not forget to meet me."

*P*urple velvet, purple larkspur, and a single rose (right) say, "I love your passion and your lightness."

offer them to a monarch," begins a charming nineteenth-century book of garden poetry.

Indeed flowers were so precious to our great-grandmothers that a single blossom given by one person to another spoke volumes without a word being uttered. Through the language of flowers, silent messages of love and joy, of hope and passion, of sorrow and remembrance, of humility, even deceitfulness, were exchanged. All that was needed was a little book to translate the secret meaning of the petals and blossoms, branches and boughs into human thoughts and words.

The Victorians loved this sentimental and secretive language. They sent one another bouquets that spoke of hidden thoughts they were too shy to speak out loud. In the days before telephones, entire dialogues transpired between lovers who dropped a flower or two beneath a loved one's window or left a few carefully

chosen blossoms in a basket on a park bench! Even parlor games were based on the language of flowers.

Today we still send bouquets for the important occasions of life—births, birthdays, weddings and anniversaries, funerals, promotions, or just to mark any special day. But we select our flowers by what is available, what is pretty, or what we think the receiver would especially enjoy. Why not revive the custom of sending a secret message when you send flowers?

How meaningful it would be if a bride took the time to in-

(the flower of love) and you are saying, "My message is one of love."

Combine an iris with a spray of purple velvet (for wisdom) to send when you have been given good advice by someone to say, in the language of flowers, "My message is you were wise." Be imaginative and create your own messages.

So that you may make your own bouquets, tussie-mussies, and flower games shown in these pages, here, from a variety of sources, are many flowers, herbs, and greens and the meanings they have become associated with through the years. Some flowers have one-word associations. Other flowers suggest whole phrases. Considering the wide variety of flowers and plants there are throughout the world it is little wonder that entire books are devoted to the language of flowers. The ones given here are those we most frequently find in our own gardens, in the woods, or at florists and nurseries.

clude a special, heartfelt message in her bridesmaids' bouquets. How lovely it would be if, when sending a special present to a friend, with your card you sent a spray of flowers that symbolized the true sentiment behind your gift. With the choice of beautiful silk flowers available today you could tie your message to the bow and ship it cross-country.

We in the twentieth century can create our own language of flowers and adapt the Victorians' language to suit our own purposes. For example, the iris means "message." Why not let it mean "my message is"? Put an iris with a rose

A broken flower symbolizes a parting or goodbye. The broken daisy combined with the pansy (above left), says, "I must leave, but remember me."

*I*n combination an iris and a rose (above) carries the most important message of love.

*T*he iris and purple velvet (left) speak of wisdom.

Alyssum	*Worth beyond beauty*	Chrysanthemum, yellow	*Slighted love*
Amaryllis	*Splendid beauty*	Clematis	*Mental beauty*
Anemone	*Forsaken*	Clover, four-leaved	*Be mine*
Apple blossoms	*Fame speaks him great and good*	Clover, red	*Industry*
Asters	*Variety*	Clover, white	*Think of me*
Autumnal leaves	*Melancholy*	Cornflower	*Delicacy*
Azaleas	*Temperance*	Cowslip	*Winning grace*
Bachelors button	*Celibacy*	Crocus	*Abuse not*
Basil	*Hatred*	Crocus, spring	*Youthful gladness*
Bay leaf	*I change but in death*		
Begonia	*Deformity*		
Bittersweet	*Truth*		
Bluebell	*Constancy*		
Borage	*Bluntness*		
Box	*Stoicism*		
Broom	*Humility*	Cyclamen	*Diffidence*
Bundle of reeds	*Music*	Cypress	*Death, despair, mourning*
Buttercups	*Riches*	Daffodil	*Unrequited love*
Butterfly weeds	*Let me go*	Daffodil, great yellow	*Chivalry*
Cactus	*Warmth*	Dahlia	*Instability*
Camellia, red japonica	*Unpretending excellence*	Daisy	*Innocence and hope*
Camellia, white	*Perfected loneliness*	Dandelion	*Rustic oracle*
Campanula	*Aspiring*	Daphne	*Glory*
Candytuft	*Indifference*	Dead leaves	*Sadness*
Canterbury bells	*Acknowledgment*	Dogwood	*Durability*
Carnation, red	*Alas! For my poor heart!*	Elder	*Zealousness*
Carnation, striped	*Refusal*	Elm	*Dignity*
Carnation, yellow	*Disdain*	Evergreen	*Poverty*
Cardinal flower	*Distinction*	Evening primrose	*Silent love*
Cedar	*Strength*	Everlasting pea	*Lasting pleasure*
Champignion	*Suspicion*	Fern	*Sincerity*
Cherry blossom	*Insincerity*	Fig	*Argument*
Chickweed	*Rendezvous*	Flax	*Fate*
Chrysanthemum, red	*I love*	Fleur-de-luce	*Fire*
Chrysanthemum, white	*Truth*	Forget-me-not	*True love*
		Foxglove	*Insincerity*
		Gardenia	*Refinement*

THE LANGUAGE

Geranium	*Deceit*	Marigold	*Grief*
Gillyflower	*Bonds of affection*	Mimosa	*Sensitivity*
Gladiolus	*Ready armed*	Morning glory	*Affectation*
Goldenrod	*Precaution*	Myrtle	*Love*
Grass	*Submission*	Narcissus	*Egotism*
Grape, wild	*Charity*	Oak leaves	*Bravery*
Hawthorn	*Hope*	Oleander	*Beware*
Hibiscus	*Delicate beauty*	Palm	*Victory*
Holly	*Foresight*	Pansy	*Thought*
Hollyhock	*Ambition*	Passion flower	*Faith*

OF FLOWERS

		Pennyroyal	*Flee away*
		Peony	*Shame*
		Periwinkle, blue	*Early friendship*
		Periwinkle, white	*Pleasures of memory*
		Petunia	*Your presence soothes me*
Honeysuckle	*Generous devotion and affection*	Phlox	*Unanimity*
Hyacinth	*Sport, game, play*	Poppy, red	*Consolation*
Hydrangea	*Heartlessness*	Primrose	*Early youth and sadness*
Hyssop	*Cleanliness*	Rose	*Love*
Iris	*Message*	Rosemary	*Remembrance*
Ivy	*Friendship*	Snapdragon	*Presumption*
Jasmine	*Amiability*	Snowdrop	*Hope*
Jonquil	*I desire a return of affection*	Stock	*Lasting beuty*
Juniper	*Protection*	Sunflower	*Haughtiness*
Larkspur	*Lightness*	Sweet pea	*Delicate pleasure*
Laurel	*Glory*	Thyme	*Activity or courage*
Lavender	*Distrust*	Tulip	*Charity*
Lilac, purple	*First emotions of love*	Tulip, red	*Declaration of love*
Lilac, white	*Joy of youth*	Tulip, yellow	*Hopeless love*
Lily, day	*Coquetry*	Verbena, pink	*Family union*
Lily, yellow	*Falsehood*	Verbena, white	*Pray for me*
Lily-of-the-valley	*Return of happiness*	Violet, blue	*Faithfulness*
Live oak	*Liberty*	Violet, yellow	*Rural happiness*
Lotus	*Eloquence*	Water lily	*Purity of heart*
Magnolia	*Magnificence*	White oak	*Independence*
Maple	*Reserve*	Wisteria	*Welcome, fair stranger*
		Yew	*Sorrow*
		Zinnia	*Thoughts of absent friends*

TUSSIE-MUSSIES
and More Language of Flowers

*L*arkspur, purple velvet, and tiny forget-me-nots in various hues of lavender, yellow roses with outer petals tipped in scarlet, and blush-pink sweet peas are lovely in an English silver filigree tussie-mussie set with small turquoise stones.

*T*he petallike tussie-mussie cup is just the right size for a few sprays of ixia, dianthus, and irresistible blue lace blossoms.

"Begin with a lovely yellow nasturtium for the center. Surround it with some carnations and gilloflowers to make a delicate tussie-mussie for sight and scent," John Parkinson instructed his readers in the early seventeenth century.

I never heard the term "tussie-mussie" until just a few years ago, though the English botanical writers and poets wrote of them often. But the first time I *did* hear those playful, romantic rhyming words I instinctively knew what a tussie-mussie was. It could only be the old-fashioned nosegay.

How I loved nosegays as a child . . . and as a young girl. I carried them at my piano recitals. When I think of Mrs. Bustard's Christmas recitals, I picture my green or blue velvet and white-lace-collared dress—and a red and white carnation nosegay. The nosegay was part of the total outfit. My spring recital outfit was a stiffly starched white pique dress with a pastel sash—and a pink or yellow rose nosegay.

Christmas or spring, only the dress and the particular flowers were different. The ritual was the same. When your turn came, you walked trembling to the piano, placed your nosegay on the piano top, where the music rack was down (we had to play from memory), turned, curtsied to Mrs. Bustard, your mother, and fellow students, and sat down to meet your fate.

When you finished your performance as best you could, you stood up, took the nosegay in hand, curtsied once again, and walked as fast as possible back to your seat, red-faced, in great pain, in mortal fear of your mother and Mrs. Bustard, and vowing all the way to practice, practice, practice before the next recital.

Luckily my memories of nosegays as a young lady are much more pleasant. For the formal dances, first at cotillion and later at college, we had our choice—a wrist corsage or a nosegay. Somewhere, perhaps in a wonderfully romantic movie, or in a slighty risqué play given by the local Little Theater group, or even in my dreams, I had seen a beautiful woman holding a nosegay at just the right angle in her hand that was draped around her lover's back as they danced the night away.

It was no contest. Who wanted a wrist corsage that left a mark on your arm from the too-tight rubber band and that was crushed when you forgot and stuck your arm into your coat sleeve anyway? In my old photograph album are pictures of me holding romantic gardenia nosegays (my favorite), feminine baby's breath and miniature rose nosegays, and delicate freesia and sweet pea nosegays all faithfully sent by my sweetheart. Ah, but enough reminiscing. Back to the tussie-mussies.

These days the term has become so popular we see it everywhere. Instructions on how to make tussie-mussies are

When going to a ball in the 1870s, a young lady would carry her sweet pea and forget-me-not tussie-mussie in her hand with the ring slipped around one finger. But to dance or visit with others, she would unscrew the ball at the bottom and leave the tussie-mussie holder upright on its tripod stand so the flowers would not be crushed when lying down.

A single pink rose is joined by dianthus, larkspur, and forget-me-nots in this reproduction tussie-mussie holder. The pin attached to the chain is designed to slip through the open work and hold the flowers in place.

given in books and magazines, in flower-arranging classes, even on morning TV shows. Yet every time I use the term before an audience, later several people invariably ask, "Now what did you call that dear little bouquet of flowers? Was it a tuss-muss, or a mussie-tuss, or something like that?" And everyone wants to make one.

If you wish to be faithful to the seventeenth-century tradition and let your tussie-mussie or nosegay speak for you in the language of flowers, you will find this passage written in the 1930s by Rosetta Clarkson most helpful.

A man might send a maid a nosegay composed of a dwarf sunflower (your devout adorer); Austrian rose (thou art all that's lovely); scarlet ranunculus (I am dazzled by your charm); and pelargonium quercifolium (Lady, deign to smile). A bit gaudy, to be sure, but the love-sick suitor would at least get his ideas across that way. Or he could send a red tulip (declaration of love) and jonquils (I desire a return of affection).

But tussie-mussies can also be simple and without hidden meanings—just a gathering of flowers assembled, as Parkinson said, for sight and scent. Incidentally, herbs make lovely additions

Marjorie Cheshire made this lovely and fragrant tussie-mussie as a special gift for the wedding of our good friend Pickett Guthrie's elder daughter, Kendall.

to tussie-mussies—especially rosemary, lemon verbena, and various mints— as do the floral-scented small-leafed geraniums.

To make an old-fashioned nosegay or tussie-mussie I always recommend holding your flowers and herbs in your hand as you gather and arrange them. The traditional way to make your bouquet is to put the showiest, largest flower in the center and surround it with smaller, more delicate blossoms and edge it with some airy or feathery greens. But more modern tussie-mussies using florists' flowers are just as attractive as the old-fashioned clusters of garden flower nosegays that our grandmothers made. And of course you can always follow tradition one day and be modern the next. To have the most fun with your flowers, make whatever bouquet fits your mood and personality of the moment.

Notice the holders in the illustrations. These too are called tussie-mussies and are quite popular today. I remember only prim lacy paper doilies tied with ruffly ribbons around my nosegays, but the English and Continental ladies of the eighteenth and nineteenth centuries carried their bouquets in beautiful and expensive silver filigree and hand-painted porcelain holders, or tussie-mussies. Though the authentic old ones are hard to find and quite expensive today, nice reproductions are being made that are lovely to set around, especially in a Victorian-style bedroom. They are also most suitable for brides— and piano recitals.

LOVE-LIES-BLEEDING

*L*ove-lies-bleeding! The poet Milton crowned the celestial beings in *Paradise Lost* with wreaths of this deep crimson, lush, shrublike flower. But the turn-of-the-century garden writer Alice Earle called it a "shapeless, gawky creature," and told of the old wives' tale that said if love-lies-bleeding were in a garden "the house would surely be struck with lightning." To children, its long, ghoulie-ghostie velvety fingers are intriguing. To star-crossed lovers it is the symbol of hopelessness, not heartlessness. Whether love-lies-bleeding is planted in the ground, as it is at Monticello (above), or in a planter with contrasting silver-gray dusty miller mixed in, this old-fashioned plant is fascinating.

FOOLISH FLOWERS

But there's yet another language of flowers, a humorous, playful, mirthful language—a play on words, so to speak. Of all the garden poems I read to my children, the one they loved the most was "Foolish Flowers" by Rupert Sargent Holland in *A Small Child's Book of Verse*.

We've Foxgloves in our garden;
How careless they must be
To leave their gloves out hanging
Where everyone can see!

And Bachelors leave their Buttons
In the same careless way,
If I should do the same with mine,
What would my mother say?

We've lots of Larkspurs in the Yard—
Larks only fly and sing—
Birds surely don't need spurs because
They don't ride anything!

And as for Johnny-Jump-Ups—
I saw a hornet light
On one of them the other day,
He didn't jump a mite!

Such play on words has long been a source of humor to gardeners—and not just for children's enjoyment. In the March 12, 1767, *Virginia Gazette*, this question was addressed to a Lady: "Why is a Gardener the most extraordinary man in the world?" The slightly risqué answer, in the tradition of eighteenth-century ribald wittiness, was:

Because no man has more business upon Earth, and always gives good Grounds for what he does. He commands his Thyme. He is master of his Mint, and fingers Penny-Royal. He raises his Salary every year, and it is a bad year indeed that does not produce a Plum. He meets with more Boughs than a Minister of State. He makes more Beds than the French King, and has in them more Painted Ladies; and more Genuine Roses and Lilies than are to be found at a country wake. He makes Raking his business more than his diversion, as many other Gentlemen do. He can boast more Rakes than any other Raker in the kingdom; His wife, notwithstanding, has enough Lads, Love and Hearts Ease and never wishes for weeds.... He can boast more Bleeding Hearts than your Ladyship, and more Laurels if possible than His Majesty of Prussia; but his greatest pride, and the world's greatest envy is, he can have Yew whenever he pleases.

In my own garden, a stray bachelor's button reminds me of these lines:

I used to love my garden
But now my love is dead.
For I found a Bachelor's Button
In Black-Eyed Susan's bed.

Christopher Morley

I, too, have lots of larkspurs in the yard (opposite), but I've yet to see a lark!

From Susan's black eyes come next year's flowers.

A Gift from the Garden

FLOWER PARLOR GAME

In Victorian days "parlor games" were favorite pastimes. Most of the games we read about in the turn-of-the-century books and magazines seem outdated, even silly to us. Yet some remain fun to play and are a great conversation piece.

Such a game is the one young girls of courting age played to foretell their suitor's or intended husband's personality in the language of flowers. It is such a pretty game and so humorous, it would make a delightful addition to a bridal shower or party.

Because the game was intended to be played year-round, it was suggested that painted flower cards (a talented hostess could still do that today) or "dried flowers gummed on cards" be used when fresh flowers were not in bloom. Of course today our florists have a profusion of flowers in all seasons, or you can play the game with silk flowers.

To prepare, make a bouquet of many different flowers. Use an appropriate Victorian vase to add to the charm and au-thenticity of the game. (The bouquet makes a wonderful decoration piece until the end of the party when the drawing takes place.) Have as many gift cards and envelopes as there are flowers. On each gift card write a flower's secret meaning, put it in an envelope, and punch a hole through the corner. Run a ribbon through the hole and tie it to the corresponding flower. At the party each guest then draws a flower from the bouquet and learns her paramour's "secret" character (reading it aloud of course).

Here are some suggestions for your bouquet and its message: violet, modest; white or pink hyacinth, playful; dark blue or purple hyacinth, mournful; primrose, candid; daisy, an early riser; pansy, kind and thoughtful; daffodil, daring; geranium, stupid; sprig of myrtle, devoted; marigold, rich; lily, pure; stock, hasty; pink rose, haughty; red rose, loving; tulip, proud; jasmine, amiable; foxglove, deceitful; aster, changeable; oak bough, hospitable.

"Your voiceless lips, O flowers, are living preachers— each cup a pulpit, and each leaf a book."

~

Horace Smith

Like the poetry of yesterday, old-fashioned flowers such as alyssum and calendula, roses, lilies, and clematis (clockwise from top left) remain timeless.

THE POETRY OF HERBS

$\mathcal{T}$hrough the ages, herb gardens have been spoken of as "magic gardens." Indeed, herbs have been the mainstay of the garden since earliest times. Their various fragrances, lovely appearance, and multiple uses are legendary. There are beautiful herb textures—from crinkly mint leaves to wooly lambs' ear—delicate herb colors—from pale blue

*S*tore your herbal bath and sprinkling waters in lovely bottles for a decorative touch that will refresh your spirit just as the herbs soothe your body.

*Y*ou don't have to have a sunken bathtub or skylight in your bathroom to bring elegance and the outside to your quiet time. A bubble bath with lavender water (right) is wonderful in itself. Remember to add a sprig of rosemary to make you "lusty, lively, joyful, and youngly."

rosemary to white thyme—and delicious herb fragrances—from tangy sage to citrusy lemon balm. From time immemorial herbs have had a thousand different uses.

In recent years herbs have become more and more popular as a garden staple. Yet some people think you must have spacious country grounds to have room for an herb garden. But it takes only a sunny window ledge to hold a pot or two of your favorite herbs. With just a little more room you can have a most original herb garden.

Here now are a few simple and practical suggestions for using herbs while enjoying their beauty and aromas. You can use herbs you have grown yourself, or have bought especially for the pleasure of making these items, or to give as gifts. In today's busy world, few of us have the extra hours to get involved in difficult crafts and projects. Yet we may yearn to make little objects as an expression of our personalities and as a creative outlet. These projects truly are uncomplicated and they take only a few minutes to prepare.

Herbal Waters

Herbal water is lovely to look at and a delight to use either for your personal bathing enjoyment or to add a gentle scent to your linens.

After a long day spent toiling in the garden, what could be more relaxing than a hot bath, especially when you add some of your favorite herbs for a sweet aroma. Simply tie a handful of herbs of your choice into a square of cheesecloth. Use a ribbon long enough to loop the herb bag over the tap. The flowing hot water will release the wonderful fragrance into your bath. Herbalists tell us the most refreshing herbs are lavender flowers, rose buds and rose petals, and chamomile, but any combination will do.

Your bed and bath linens will be outdoors fresh when they are sprinkled with a little herbal sprinkling water before being pressed or even dried in the clothes dryer. To a cup of rose water (or rose water and glycerin) bought at the drugstore or herb shop, add 3 or 4 sprigs of fresh lavender in a clean jar and seal. Keep in a warm place (near a heat vent in the winter) for two or three weeks. The warmth releases the scent. Strain the herbs out and put the lovely pastel-

colored water in attractive jars and bottles. There will be enough herb water to put in small perfume bottles to decorate your dressing table, as well as in other bottles or jars to use for bathing and as sprinkling water.

Herb Sachets

Another way to keep your linens and lingerie fresh is to make little herb bags. You can buy these in the stores, of course, but nothing could be simpler to make at only a fraction of the cost. Further, you can select the outer cloth to fit your tastes and moods. In the olden days wealthy ladies would make herb bags from expensive laces, satins, and ribbons while the less well-to-do ladies used checks and gingham scraps left over from their sewing.

Cut squares of fabric approximately 8" x 8" (you can make yours larger or smaller) with either straight scissors or pinking shears. Using dried herbs, put either all of one herb or a mixture of

Herb sachets made from your own choice of fabric and color will blend with your distinctive decorating style.

complementary herbs in the center of the square. Gather the fabric together and tie it with a pretty ribbon. If you wish to, you can trim the border of the fabric square in lace or hemstitch it.

Should you wish to dry your own herbs, the microwave makes this a snappy process. Wash and thoroughly wipe off the herbs. Put a layer of herbs on a brown paper bag (a lunch sack is perfect). Cover with a strip of wax paper. Put in the microwave on high for three minutes. Then rotate the bag half way. Microwave on high for another ten minutes. This expedient method dries them instantly while preserving their color and fragrance.

Cheesecloth, simple gingham, elegant satins, and herbs are all it takes to make charming herb sachets.

Herbal Vinegars

No discussion of uses for herbs would be complete without mentioning how they can add pleasure to your dining experience. I know how much time cooking preparation takes. Our best intentions often become a source of frustration when we become rushed or encounter untold interruptions in the time we set aside for worry-free kitchen fun. Here is a no-fail and very pretty herbal vinegar you can make in no time and use on the take-out salads you pick up after a long day or add to a store-bought vinegar. And remember, it will make a special gift as well.

Choose either from your garden or the store any edible flowers you may find—pansies, primroses, violets, and the like. Pick only the blossoms, totally removing the stems. Carefully wash and dry them. Gather glass bottles of various shapes and sizes. I prefer the dusty old bottles found at the corner antique shop, but there are wonderful shapes and sizes in the stores as well. The one criterion is that the opening and neck be wide enough to drop the flower blossoms into. Simply alternate layers of white sugar and flowers until the bottle is 3/4 full. Then pour in white wine vinegar up to the shoulder of the bottle and replace the cork. Leave for two to three weeks in a sunny spot. The vinegar will slowly change to a lovely pastel color. Herbal vinegars can be used alone to be added to your favorite sauces and dressings to enhance their flavor. (Incidentally, when I

$\mathscr{A}$nyone can combine the tops of a few spring blooming primroses, sugar, and unflavored white vinegar to make a lovely herbal vinegar. And a spray or two of lavender adds a delicate touch of flavor and uniqueness to your store-bought bottle of olive oil.

was making my herbal vinegar it was so lovely that I got the idea to pop a few primroses into a bottle, pour in some herbal water, and make my bath herbal water even more cheerful and inviting to use.)

Another pleasing flavor to enhance foods comes from the flowers of the lavender plant. Simply add a few sprigs of lavender to a bottle of virgin olive oil. The hint of lavender adds a wonderfully distinct taste to sauces and dressings made with this olive oil. Like the vinegar, the oil must also mature in the sun for a few weeks.

Herb Table

I first saw an herb table when I was visiting Barbara Thomas in her Seattle home. Her small, city garden was magical. Little figures peeked out from behind lush green hostas and ferns. A small reflecting pool was made twice its size by tall, vertical mirrors at one end. Reflections of her bountiful, forest-green garden shone beautifully in the mirrors while the graceful white clouds rolling across the pale blue sky were captured in the rippling water. But most interesting of all was her herb table, a grand idea for the small garden that hasn't room to hold both herbs *and* flowers, or the apartment with a patio or balcony only large enough for a table and chairs. It's a great idea for Southern beaches, where the sandy soil and elements make it almost impossible to have a garden.

To make the table you can buy a new one, of course, but you can salvage an old table that has a broken top or pick up a used one inexpensively at a yard sale. I chose one with a mesh top that I had on hand. This is easiest because the table was ready for "planting."

But if you use a table that originally had a glass top you can make the foundation for the herbs by securing a couple of layers of chicken wire laid one on top of the other to the table ledge to span the area where the top used to be. Measure your tabletop and then cut two pieces of chicken wire, allowing an extra four inches or so to overlap all around. Cut one piece a little larger than the first so it can be staggered over the first layer. This way the size of the holes will be minimized and the foundation will be made stronger. Use strong wire to secure these mesh layers.

Place one layer of chicken wire across the table, stretching it taut. Attach this layer to the table by rolling the extra wire around the table ledge and securing it in several places with lengths of wire. Attach the second layer over the first, staggering the mesh so that a uniform pattern of smaller holes is formed. Secure it with wire. With the top in place, next overlap several strips of wax paper or brown parchment paper on the mesh. Be generous. You will trim the edges off after the top is planted.

Next spread a layer of sandbox sand purchased from your garden supply store all across the top of the table. Decide whether you want to use the table just for growing herbs or if you would actually like to eat on it, as I elected to do. If you wish to use your table as a real dining table, remember to put down a plate in the planting process so you will leave sufficient room. This section can be left unplanted, with the sand showing, or covered with a moss "placemat." Then, with your hands, build the sand up slightly at the center. If you want to make places for plates, mark those off as shown in the photograph of the table "in progress." Remember, though, mistakes can always be corrected and you may want to just experiment at first. Arrange the herb plants for a variety of textures, heights, and colors. Place the tallest plants at the center with the lower, bushier ones toward the front. Don't be afraid to shake the potting soil from the roots of the herbs as you take them out of their pots. The roots will spread into the soil of the surrounding plants and down into the sand. (At the end, when you have the plants arranged as you want them, you may want to add some additional potting soil in bare places to hold the plants in place and give them extra dirt to grow in. This can easily be covered by sheet moss.)

While making your arrangement, use a few small- to medium-sized pebbles to anchor the plants in place and add interest to your woodland scene. If you like, add touches of color by planting a few flowers. I particularly like marigolds. In the sixteenth century these were a favored flower-herb for both cooking and medicines. And for a decorative touch, why not add a small garden ornament. Here you see one of my little

COMFORT GARDEN SALAD

A lovely accompaniment to any luncheon is this tasty, healthy and easy to prepare Comfort Garden Salad. Not only should it be made the day before—always a help in these busy days—its green, white, and golden colors perfectly complement those of the herb table, and the dill can be pinched from your tabletop garden.

To prepare, peel and cut into bite-size pieces 1 bunch of broccoli and 1 head of cauliflower. Put in a large bowl and combine these with 4 thinly sliced scallions, ½ cup chopped pitted ripe olives, and 2 cups shredded sharp Cheddar cheese. Prepare the dressing by mixing together with a wire whisk 1 cup storebought poppy seed dressing, 3 tablespoons Southern Comfort whiskey, 1 teaspoon celery seeds, and 1 teaspoon chopped dill weed. Pour the dressing over the vegetables and lightly toss. Cover tightly and refrigerate the Comfort Garden Salad for one day before serving.

bunnies having a feast, but you might prefer a small child or angel statue. One of the charming little seated angel statues so popular these days would be most attractive perched on the edge of the table. I can visualize an herb table with an Oriental motif made by using a bonsai plant as the center focal point and having charming small mud figurines and a few tiny chrysanthemum plants throughout. In short, an herb table can be anything you imagine it to be.

Finish the arrangement by packing wet sheet moss along the table rim. If you have used a chicken-wire top, you will want to cover the exposed wires around the edge with the moss.

For maintenance, tend it as you would pots of herbs on your window ledge or an herb garden. Sprinkle and/or mist it with water every few days or more often as needed, and every month or so add a little liquid fertilizer to your water. Gusty winds, a scorching sun, and hard rain play havoc with the herb table, so it is best kept in a sheltered place. And the layers of paper will eventually rot, which is why you want to put several strips down when making the table. Yet this is such a fun idea and so easy to create that replanting it only gives you a chance to try a new design or different herbs. Pinch off dead leaves and blooms and, when needed, replace any drooping plants. And don't forget to use the herbs for cooking, to garnish a meal, and in your flower arrangements.

Suggested herbs: Your nursery or herb shop can give you additional recommendations, but here is a partial list of the herbs and plants used in the table shown on page 77:

german chamomile
lemon variegated thyme
mole plant
hypoestes (pink splash)
curry plant
dill
purple sage
creeping rosemary
pot marigold
basil
parsley
lamb's ear
dusty miller
scented geranium

*H*erb gardens, like these at the Flag Fork Herb Farm outside Frankfort, Kentucky, are as colorful as any flower garden.

"There's a difference between plants,
as there is between people!"

Hans Christian Andersen

FAMILY GARDENS

*M*y grandmother was like her garden, quiet and content. Her flawless complexion was as smooth as the petals of her favorite pink cabbage roses. Her gentle laughter was as bright as the early summer buttercups that we picked on our Sunday walks in the park. Her always-fragrant scent was as fresh as the perfume of the Sweet Betsy

I spent many happy hours with my Mamma in her lovely southern garden.

"But of the flowers that deck the field, Or grace the garden of the cot, Though others richer perfumes yield, The sweetest is forget-me-not."

~

New Monthly Magazine

buds we crushed between our fingers in early June. Her smiling eyes were as blue as the delicate larkspur faces we pinched off and pretended were miniature puppets in the shade of the late afternoon. Even her flowered voile dresses with round pearl buttons were woven images of the garden she grew and loved.

Mamma, as I called my mild-mannered, ladylike Southern grandmother, worked religiously in her garden. I can still see her, a full apron covering her dress, clippers in hand, bringing armfuls of frilly peonies and sprays of mock oranges into the house. She had to tend her own flowers. She didn't have a gardener, and Papa, my grandfather, preferred fishing to gardening. There was no one else to do it. But I never once remember seeing a lock of her carefully pinned-

back silver hair out of place or a smudge of dirt on her rosy cheeks, much less under her fingernails.

Mamma's garden was as neat as she was. At the front of the house well-trained ivy that never ventured into the manicured grass lawn covered a rock wall. At the side of the house a refined, perfectly graduated garden bloomed from mid-February until early November.

In each season a thick, low border marked its edge. Early spring candytuft and pansies bloomed first. These were replaced by bunches of dwarf marigolds for the hot summer months. In September, my favorite, fuzzy-faced, bluish ageratum took over. Behind them stair steps of pink columbines and lavendar iris, yellow zinnias and red bee balm, rusty-orange chrysanthemums and off-white

*O*ld-fashioned gardens have a sweet charm that comes from textures and colors layered together. A wall or fence—never intended to keep anyone out—makes a beautiful background.

*T*he late afternoon sun nourishes the low-growing green hydrangea blossoms that will soon turn blush pink.

A leisurely
stroll through
a boxwood
garden—a stolen
snooze beneath
the shade of
bending boughs—
what lovely ways
to while away a
summer's day!

Garden beauty
is everywhere,
from a profusion
of blooms to a
single water lily
in a neighbor-
hood garden.

feverfew were carefully arranged for height and color. At the back was a hedge that remained green year round. Order reigned in my grandmother's garden.

How differently I remember my mother in her garden. How different was the garden itself!

Almost every afternoon Mother toiled in her garden. For the task she donned baggy gabardine pants, an oversized "smock," and a pair of lace-up skin shoes

Cabbage roses (below) and profusely blooming herbs and flowers (opposite) evoke gentle memories of Mamma's garden.

she must have had for twenty years (she always told me they were too good to discard). On a hook Daddy had put by the basement door, the exit from our tall house to the terraced garden, hung a large straw hat intended to shade her fair complexion from the sun. Mother couldn't be bothered with it, or with the chamois gloves my grandmother had given her to protect her hands, though her freckles and wrinkles became more noticeable each year. Bareheaded and gloveless, she dug in her capricious rock garden on all fours, a lock of reddish blonde hair always in her eyes.

Nothing about my mother's garden resembled Mamma's garden. Lush mounds of pink and yellow weeping lantana cascaded over the uneven earth. Fingers of purple verbena crawled around the jagged corners of striated stones Daddy had chiseled into just the right shape. Fiery crimson and scarlet portulaca, happy in the dry, red dirt, ran rampant over the retaining wall and burst into full bloom in the midday sun.

In cooler shady nooks sheltered by large boulderlike rocks, sprays of graceful begonias, delicate, soulful bleeding hearts, fragrant, feathery dianthus, and ever-faithful forget-me-nots were quite at home. Carefully positioned patches of green broad-leafed hostas and spidery ferns dug up in the woods tied the kaleidoscope of colors together.

Like her garden, my mother was full of contradictions. She was sharp-witted and outspoken, yet she was generous to a fault and ever-forgiving. Her pale blue eyes belied her hearty laugh. In her heart she had room for all manner of human-kind, but like many of her generation, she had prejudices she could never over-come.

Often, when I am working in my own garden, I enjoy remembering my grandmother and my mother and the gardens they loved. Soon I see them, each in her own way, there by me in the garden.

Mamma, her dress falling in graceful folds, moves among the roses gathering an afternoon bouquet. Mother, a smudge of dirt on her forehead where she has swept her hair out of her eyes, is transplanting an enormous canary-yellow nasturtium so it can comfortably crawl down the rocks for all to admire.

My visions are not sad. They are rich and real. They add beauty and meaning to my garden. They give me an understanding of myself.

In my mind's eye, my wished-for garden is as charming and gracious as Mamma's garden. It is neat, well groomed, and serene, just the way I see myself in the antique gold-leaf mirror above my dressing table.

But glancing down at my dirt-stained knees and ragged fingernails, I see my mother's reflection. And even if I didn't want to admit it, my overly ambitious, spontaneous, and exuberant garden is evidence no mirror can hide.

"Whoever makes a garden
Has never worked alone...."
Douglas Malloch

*Lantana
(above), bleeding
hearts and forget-
me-nots, and
phlox (opposite,
top and bottom)—
flowers I learned
to love in my-
mother's and
grandmother's
gardens.*

AN HOUR IN
THE GARDEN

*"All my hurts
My garden-spade can heal."*
Ralph Waldo Emerson

~

I can hear my mother now, saying to my father some thirty-five years ago as we drove down the old state highway, a paved, but little-traveled road, "We're coming up on that patch of phlox around this bend—now's the time to dig it up. Slow, now. Over there." She would always be right.

She had a sixth sense for where flowers grew along the side of the road, whether they had been scattered there by birds and the wind, or were the sole remnants of a long-ago front yard. Together my parents would get out of the car, taking the rain-rusted trowel out of the trunk, and head toward the patch of phlox, invisible to all but their eyes.

My job usually was to carry the day-old newspaper to wrap the plants in. And no matter how late it was when we got home that night, the phlox—or whatever flower my mother had begged, borrowed or stolen that day—had to be put into the rock garden and watered. Then I'd promptly forget the day's events until months later, when Mother would remark, "Ah, that phlox is a little darker pink than I thought it would be. But it certainly is perfect next to the candytuft. Remind me to tell your father we must dig some more."

Though Mother loved her flowers and studied most diligently the various horticulture magazines she subscribed to, I always knew that to her, flowers were only metaphors for the larger lessons of life. In her garden I learned more philosophy than from being in any classroom.

Many an afternoon when I came home from grammar school I would find my mother, not playing bridge—the fashionable thing women did in the early 1950s—but kneeling on the linoleum pad Daddy had cut out for her to keep from soiling the already grass-stained knees of her gabardine slacks, digging, bare-handed, in her rock garden. While she planted and transplanted, weeded and pruned, I'd tell her about the day's events.

"Margaret Ann pushed her way in front of me at lunch today," I would remark, still angry.

"Remember, she's got an older brother," Mother would say gently. "I imagine there are times when she has to push to get her way at home. I'm sure she just forgot she was at school." Then Mother would add, "Oh, look at the littlest pansy plant over there. The tall ones with the big faces and the thick stalks are pushing it out. I think I'll move the sweet little

LADY ASTOR'S ROSES

Nancy and Irene Langhorne were born in the late nineteenth century in an attractive but modest apartment house in my hometown of Danville, Virginia. Irene became the beautiful Gibson Girl, America's ideal image of grace, beauty, and charm as captured on canvas by her famous artist-husband Charles Dana Gibson. Equally beautiful Nancy married Waldorf Astor, one of the world's richest men, and became Lady Astor, the first woman to sit in the House of Commons—a position she earned by popular vote. In 1922 Lady Astor returned to Danville where, after a talk to the town's school children, she presented them with 2,000 rose bushes, telling them they should cultivate their minds the way roses are cultivated. Upon hearing this lovely story, Danville historian Patricia Brachman searched until she found four of the original plants still thriving some seventy years later. Frances Field, who heard Lady Astor that day, has lovingly nourished her "Lady Astor" rose ever since. Today it grows only a few yards from the house where I grew up.

one over here by the Johnny-jump-ups where it can be the biggest one." She didn't have to say another word.

One early spring morning—I must have been about eight or nine—when I came down to breakfast in a favorite Christmas-red and hunter-green gingham blouse tucked into my new pink-and-gray plaid skirt, Mother cheerfully remarked, "You've so many bright colors on I think I should plant you in my garden rather than send you off to school!" I went upstairs and changed my skirt.

Our dinner-table conversation often included some casual reference to the garden, though it was seldom the topic of conversation.

"Have you seen dear Mrs. Brown lately?" Mother might begin. "I thought of her today when I was pulling the wild morning glories out from around the climbing roses. She's not had an easy life." Though Mother never compared Mrs. Brown to the long-suffering but proud roses, in my mind's eye I immediately knew those morning glories were her wild teenage daughters who ran away and didn't tell their mother where they were going until they were hours away from home.

Now that I have reached the age my mother was then, I understand that my mother's garden was her sanctuary. The place where, as Wordsworth said, "...the heavy and the weary weight / Of all this unintelligible world / Is lightened." The place where she worked out her own problems and those of the world, as she saw them, while she tended her plants

DAFFODIL, JONQUIL, OR NARCISSUS?

*W*hen admiring a gloriously colorful and fragrant array of white and yellow ruffly spring flowers, have you ever stopped and wondered whether they are daffodils, jonquils, or narcissus—(narcissi to be absolutely correct)? I always call them "daffodil" because daffodil is such a nice old-fashioned sounding name. Anyway that's what Mamma always called them too.

To find the correct name I went to the pages of *Daffodils, Outdoors and In* by Carey E. Quinn. According to Quinn, taxonomists, the scientists who classify plants, call them narcissus, the genus name. But, he writes, "in common practice in the catalogues of the world, and in most current garden magazines, they are called 'daffodils.' The words 'narcissus' and 'daffodil' mean exactly the same thing."

But where, I wondered, does "jonquil" fit in? Quinn obviously wondered the same, for he continues, "There are a great many people who would call all daffodils 'jonquils,' and I cannot even guess where this custom came from because it is completely erroneous. The jonquil is merely one of eleven families of daffodils—a little multi-flowered sweet scented item—and actually constitutes only a very small part of the whole daffodil family."

Knowing the correct name, you now may let the very musical, almost whimsical word "daffodil" roll off your tongue with confidence and assurance.

"Daffodils bloom when the bareness of winter is still in the trees."

~

Elizabeth Lawrence

A Gift from the Garden

HOMEMADE FLOWER PRESS

Many of my fondest garden moments are not spent in the garden at all. Rather they come as little surprises when I open a book and find a pressed buttercup, fern leaf, or my favorite—a four-leaf clover. I once even bought a used book I didn't need simply because when I opened it, a half-plucked daisy was pressed on the page beside a photograph of a wild daisy. How could I resist it? When I got home, I found other lovely pressed flowers and even personal notations about gardening among the pages.

One early spring day last year I found the biggest four-leaf clover I've ever seen. I proudly showed my prize to Liza Vaughan and told her I was going to press and keep it forever. She then told me how when she was little and her family visited her grandparents, she, her brother, and her grandmother spent hours plopped down in a clover patch swatting at pesky bumblebees while searching for those magical four-leaf good-luck symbols. They always came away with a handful of four-leaf clovers, and at the end of the day would sit at grandmother's bridge table to carefully place their bounty of good-luck promises between the cardboard pages of a homemade flower press.

Although you can now purchase flower presses at garden and gift shops, making your own press, as Liza's grandmother did, is more personal. All you need are two small pieces of 1/4" plywood cut the same size and sanded smooth (your flower press can be any size you wish—or any shape), four screws with wing nuts, some cardboard, and pretty color tissue, blotting, or wrapping paper.

Stack the two pieces of plywood together. In each corner of these plywood sheets drill a small hole the right size for your screws. Decorate the top piece of plywood any way you wish—paint it, decoupage it, or even cover it in fabric. Cut six pieces of cardboard and twelve pieces of the paper in the shape of the plywood pieces, but about 1/8" smaller all around. Cut off their corners where the screws will hold the press in place.

To assemble your press, simply layer the tissue and cardboard between the plywood covers. First lay down a piece of the paper. Next, layer a piece of the cardboard and two pieces of the paper, followed by another piece of cardboard. End with a piece of the pretty paper and the cover.

To press your flowers, snip off any unwanted stems or leaves and put a blossom between the two pieces of paper on one of the cardboard layers, beginning with the bottom layer. If you put more than one blossom per layer, be sure to place flowers of equal thickness on each layer; keep the flowers from touching or overlapping. Reassemble the press, tightening the wing nuts for a snug fit. Keep your press in a temperate, dry atmosphere. Every few days tighten the wing nuts a little more. After eight to twelve weeks your flowers should be thoroughly dried.

and flowers, day in and day out. In her garden, Mother put life into perspective.

For, you see, people who garden do see things differently. They see life differently.

In solitude they take the time to pause, to reflect, to sort through problems big and small. In a garden people see the balance between the strong and the weak, the newborn and the time-weary. People who garden learn when to dig up and transplant, when it's just the right time to pinch a sprig off to spur new growth, and when it's better to let things well enough alone. They come to realize that overfeeding and overwatering are just as harmful as neglect. They know each day has it beginning and its ending, and that some days the dark will come before the daylight tasks can be completed. And most important, they find that time teaches them that all too often, no matter how they try, unannounced and unforeseen forces—the wind, a storm, even a neighbor's stray dog or cat—can undo all the toil and love one person has put into a garden.

But when such things happen, people who garden also see tomorrow's marigolds and zinnias and next year's larkspur and irises—and are ready to start anew.

~

My parents moved away from my childhood house and garden in 1963. Often I drive past it, or even when I just think of it happenstance, so to speak, I remember this poem by Margaret Widdemer and hope other children have played, and will play, in my mother's garden.

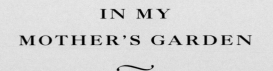

IN MY MOTHER'S GARDEN
~

There were many flowers in my mother's garden,
Sword-leaved gladiolas, taller far than I,
Sticky-leaved petunias, pink and purple flaring,
Velvet-painted pansies smiling at the sky;

Scentless portulacas crowded down the borders,
White and scarlet-petalled, rose and satin-gold,
Clustered sweet alyssum, lacy-white and scented,
Sprays of gray-green lavender to keep 'til you were old.

In my mother's garden were green-leaved hiding places,
Nooks between the lilacs—oh, a pleasant place to play!
Still my heart can hide there, still my eyes can dream it,
Though the long years lie between and I am far away.

When the world is hard now, when the city's clanging
Tires my eyes and tires my heart and dust lies everywhere,
I can dream the peace still of the soft wind's blowing,
I can be a child still and hide my heart from care.

Lord, if still that garden blossoms in the sunlight,
Grant that children laugh there now among its green and gold—
Grant that little hearts still hide its memoried sweetness,
Locking one bright dream away for light when they are old!

Margaret Widdemer

"When the birds are gone, and their warm fields
Return no more, where, then, is paradise?"

"Sunday Morning," Wallace Stevens

THE INVISIBLE GARDENER

*D*addy and I were standing at the kitchen window watching the birds come to the freshly filled bird feeder.

"I want you to watch how the blue jay eats the sunflower seed," Daddy said matter-of-factly. "Most of the other birds, the sparrows and the purple finches, pick up a seed, shuck off the shell with their beaks, spit the shell out, and eat the meat. But the blue jay puts his seed between his talons and pecks at the shell until it falls away. Then he eats the meat. Now the way I figure it, the blue jay must not have as much control over his beak as the other birds do. Look, here comes one now. Watch carefully."

Daddy was right. The blue jay picked up a single sunflower seed, held it in his

The exotically plumaged blue jay picks up a single seed, positions it between his claws and the ledge of the bird feeder, and hammers away at the shell until he finds the tasty morsel inside.

bill, and tossed his head around until he had the seed just right so he could carefully position it between his claws. With the seed pinned between his claws and the ledge of the bird feeder, the jay began hammering away at the sunflower seed. When he had loosened the shell from around the kernel, he kicked it aside and then devoured the morsel he had worked so hard to get.

Only an engineer would have observed how the blue jay and other birds eat their food to begin with, to say nothing of concluding that there is a biological difference in birds' "beak control."

If I, on the other hand, had wanted to call someone's attention to a blue jay on the bird feeder, my observations surely would have been something like, "Look at that handsome blue jay! See how erect he holds his regal head. Do you notice how his wings are striped with black and tipped with white to make the brilliant blue plumage all the brighter?"

Not Daddy. His whole life, my father has been interested in how things work and figuring out how to make them better. He had all the right ingredients to complement my mother's more romantic and flamboyant nature. Her flowers never would have been so beautiful without Daddy. He was the one with the patience, the strength, and the knowledge to build the foundation for my mother's showcase of a garden. Mother's rock garden is the first thing I remember him building. The way it came to be says everything about him.

When we moved into our house on Marshall Terrace the summer of 1947, there was a grape arbor right outside our back door made of large totem-pole–like rock columns. The rest of the yard was planted in fruit trees—apple trees, a flowering peach, and the biggest walnut tree I ever saw. I can only speculate about why this little orchard was in the middle of town. I never knew the people who had lived in the house before us and they are now long gone. The husband was a tobacconist. (Back in the 1940s and '50s the welcoming sign at the Danville, Virginia, city limits proclaimed, "Home of the World's Largest Tobacco Market!")

His wife was an artist. I have wondered if she might have used their beautiful boughs, colorful fruit, and graceful forms for her paintings.

That summer while Mother and Daddy's attention was focused on the inside of the house, I was ecstatic playing in my own outdoor fairyland filled with tiny green grapes that grew from little beads into fat, juicy purple balls and streaked yellow and red apples that both the bees and I loved. But oh! the arbor with its dark, leafy canopy! What fantastic adventures awaited me! I would climb the cragged rocks as high as I could, three or four rocks' worth, and enter another world. One day I was an Indian princess looking for approaching cowboys on the horizon. The next day I was a breathtakingly beautiful damsel trapped in the Arabian desert waiting to be rescued and, of course, "deflowered"—though I didn't know what the term meant. I just knew something deeply mysterious and wonderful would happen when I was rescued.

Two things happened that summer. First I got worms from eating the apples and the grapes—an incident that brought terrible embarrassment to my mother. Next, I fell off the grape arbor, taking a few of the stones with me. I wasn't hurt badly, but when Daddy checked out the columns and found they were close to falling down, he knocked them down with his sledgehammer. That took care of the wormy grapes and I was given strict orders not to eat any more apples.

But there was now a huge pile of rocks in the backyard. They had to serve

some purpose. They couldn't be wasted. That is how my mother's dazzlingly beautiful terraced rock garden came to be— *and* the steps, *and* the rock partition that divided the top yard from the bottom yard and formed the space that became a beautiful rose garden, *and* the wall with the glass front that held a tiny goldfish pond.

Mother selected the flowers and then planned the rock garden. She even

After a daring leap from a tree limb and a precarious slide down the bird feeder rope, this bushy-tailed squirrel clutches the roof, get his balance, and then settles down to eat.

Experience has shown you might as well give up trying to keep the squirrels off the bird feeder. But why not find a little humor in the situation and provide the squirrels their own little benches and a delicious ear of corn?

weeded it, but Daddy built the foundation and prepared the earth. He turned the soil over at exactly the right time, adding peat moss and manure so Mother could have the largest, most colorful, and bountiful blooms imaginable.

Their next addition was a compost, or mulch, pile—which in those days wasn't yet considered organic gardening. It became quite a project. Daddy did it all. He drove the stakes into the ground at the far end of the yard past the apple trees and nailed chicken wire to them. Each day he carried out the table scraps, eggshells, carrot and potato peelings, and of course the coffee grounds that had been saved in a gray galvanized bowl on the screened-in kitchen porch. Once or twice a week, to cover the decaying food, he used a long-handled pitch fork to toss leaves into the compost pile from a huge leaf pile he had raked together throughout the year. In the spring and fall he would haul the rotted compost in

an old rusted wheelbarrow up to the rock garden to enrich the earth.

"How do you do it?" Mother's garden club friends asked. "It's just the mulch from Langdon's wonderful compost pile," she would reply, as if there were no work involved.

One day, though, the compost pile took on a new meaning to me. Mother, a strawberry blonde, had, on occasion, a redhead's temper. My father, on the other hand, never raised his voice. For whatever reason, Mother got terribly mad at Daddy, so mad she said to him, "I'm going to kill you. Furthermore, nobody is going to miss you. They won't even be able to find your body because I'm going to bury you in your damn compost pile!"

"That will be just fine with me," Daddy rejoined. "At least then I'll be some good to somebody. When I've rotted away at least I'll fertilize your flowers." I never looked at the compost pile again that I didn't wonder if you really could hide a dead body in it!

Of course I later realized that at the core of my father's immediate, pragmatic response to Mother's meaningless threat was his philosophy about life. Despite years of living in the South, my father never lost his New England puritanical sense of life's duties. His responsibility was to justify his presence on earth. Even fun and enjoyment had to have some purpose to it—which is why Daddy gardened rather than played golf, even though for the past thirty years he has lived within walking distance of a golf course. To him it just wouldn't be right to hit a ball into a hole, an activity that, to his way of thinking, gives nothing back to the world. Yet Daddy has always had unfaltering faith in the world and the goodness of mankind.

And, as was the custom back then, my father was the disciplinarian. On the only occasion I can remember when some discipline other than being sent to my room or having to turn my light out early was necessary (I'll admit it, I was a goody-goody), Daddy took me down to the basement.

I was absolutely terrified. But our basement was no dungeon. It was the

"mud room" where gardening clothes, tools, flower containers, bulbs, and house plants were kept. Green, bushy ferns that needed trimming back or some extra care were hung from hooks Daddy had made from coat hangers. On the windowsill were bright purple, magenta, and white African violets—*the* fashionable indoor flower of the time. In a corner protected from drafts was a thirty-plus-year-old night-blooming sirius we lovingly called "Christ in the Manger" whose blossoms open for only one night and then harbors a miniature scene that truly does resemble Christ in the manger.

*A*n island of colorful blossoms provides a protective thicket for the residents of this charming birdhouse.

A beautiful church motif birdhouse stands tall (far left) on the spacious grounds of the Hagley Museum, Wilmington, Delaware.

*T*hese days birdhouses come in every conceivable variety including cheerfully painted vine-covered country cottages (left).

*W*hen the bluebird population around Prospect Hill, North Carolina, was dwindling, a local resident, Roger Williams, began putting up bluebird houses along fences that line farms and pasture lands (far left).

*T*here are even "decorator" birdhouses for solariums (left).

*S*andy McGregor has created a neighborhood of birdhouses, such as this Swiss "chalet" (right), Maine "country cottage" (far right), red farmyard barn (below left), and racquet club (below right), in her Charlottesville, Virginia, yard.

*I*nside a Carmel-by-the-Sea courtyard, the birds can roost in high-rise luxury.

In this atmosphere Daddy explained to me why what I had done was wrong. He asked me not to do it again "because it upset your mother." Then he proceeded to tell me how, when he was a young boy, his father had taken him down to the basement on Elm Street in Webster, Massachusetts, to discipline him. "My father told me not to do it again and then he said words I'll never forget. He told me how his father had taken him down in the cellar to discipline him and that, rather than thrashing him as they did in those days, his father explained to him why he shouldn't do it again, but then he added, 'Just remember, every generation of fathers has always thought their children were going to the dogs—that they'd all grow up to be no good at all. Well, I grew up to be just fine, and so will you.' And," my father told me in 1948, "you'll grow up to be just fine, too. Now, why don't you take one of the prettiest African violets upstairs and tell your mother you'll try to do a little better."

But back to the garden on Marshall Terrace. Mother's friends made so much over her outstanding flowers that she became interested in flower arranging. She pored over flower design books and entered flower shows.

Soon Daddy got involved. He built the box to carry Mother's arrangements of twisted bonsai tree limbs in black pottery containers to the school gym and church hall so the "line of beauty" would not be disturbed and the water wouldn't spill out. Daddy tirelessly combed the beach to gather small pebbles to place

around her bonsai and to find just the right piece of driftwood for her low-slung arrangement of galax leaves, fall asters, and long-leaf pine sprays. He tramped through poison ivy to dig the moss to pack around the base of some "naturalistic" woodland scene she dreamed up, and he was the one who carried over the poinsettias from year to year. And, when they moved, Daddy was the one who dug up some of the English boxwood and other prized plants to take with them to their new home. But the rock garden had to be left behind.

Unlike our old neighborhood, where the houses had long skinny backyards but almost touched each other, our new neighborhood had spacious, sprawling lots. Not only was there room for flowers and roses, but a little creek ran through the woods that separated one group of homes from another. Daddy immediately built a dam on the creek. Not that it was needed or served any purpose, but the creek was there and the engineer had always wanted to build his own dam.

Furthermore the woods were filled with birds. Up went the bird feeders and out came the squirrels—the scourge of every bird lover. Which, incidentally, is how we happened to be standing at the kitchen window that day.

Daddy is now in his eighties. The first few years my parents lived in that house he engineered all manner of squirrel-be-gone contraptions for his much-loved birds. None of them worked, not even the house perched at the top of an aluminum pole.

Squirrels are a favorite joke in our household. Mother gave this pottery one to Daddy as a constant reminder of how the real little animals could outsmart even a hightly educated engineer.

Daddy named the squirrel-shaped birdseed ornament the children gave him for Father's Day "Sweet Revenge."

THE DAY THE
BLACKBIRDS COME

*I*n late January hundreds of wings flapping against the wind and sky announce the arrival of the migrating blackbirds. It is an eerie sound as they circle until, as one, they swoop down upon their chosen resting place, always the top limbs of a primeval tree. They pause until some noise, unheard by you and me, causes them to scatter, circle, and perch only a few feet away, but this time on a tree turned gold by the winter sun breaking through the heavy clouds.

Mother complained that the pole was ugly. But Daddy told her the squirrels could climb a wooden pole the same way they could a tree, which is why it is pointless to hang a birdhouse in a tree unless you want the squirrels to come.

It really upset Daddy that somehow, some way, the squirrels could scoot up his aluminum pole. Then he had a brilliant idea. "I bet furniture polish will keep the squirrels off the aluminum pole!" he concluded.

Daddy put a generous coating on the aluminum stand. For a couple of days there were no intruding squirrels. Then one morning Daddy saw a little bird fly down from a tree and light on the pole rather than on the ledge already crowded with breakfasting birds. "It slid right off!" he laughed. "So did a couple of more birds." But that very afternoon, when a squirrel shimmied up the pole after a few unsuccessful tries, he said in disgust, "I should have known furniture polish would wear down just like car polish does. Anyway I certainly don't want to be responsible for any broken bird wings or legs."

My father next attempted to outsmart the squirrels by suspending a bird feeder on a thin wire—so thin a squirrel couldn't grasp it—and so far away from the house it would be out of even the most daring squirrel's reach by tree limb or off the roof of the house. He hung it out of the upstairs guest bedroom window, a full two-and-a-half-story drop to the ground. But the only way to fill the feeder was for Daddy to dangle precariously far out the window and reach out as far as he could, all the while praying he wouldn't slip or fall to his death. For a while there were no squirrels at the new feeder.

Mother thought this was grand until she found out *how* it got refilled every couple of days. After that Daddy had to wait until she was away from the house before feeding the birds. Every time Mother would see the feeder filled to the top she'd threaten to kill him. But there was no compost pile at the new house to hide his body in.

The next spring, fate—not Mother—intervened—saving Daddy from untimely death. That year, quite mysteriously, a braver, more nimble litter of baby squirrels was born. Daddy was foiled again. In no time at all, whether by leaping or flying, or a combination of both, more squirrels than ever before feasted at the bird feeder. If there was no way to keep them off he might as well accommodate the squirrels, the birds, and Mother.

Resolutely my father rerigged the bird feeder, this time on a safe pulley device. These days the squirrels come regularly to the feeder that he fills daily. So do the birds.

"You know, when the bird feeder was so far away, I never noticed all their different little habits," he said contentedly as we watched the blue jay hammer away at the sunflower seeds.

⁓

"You must not know too much, or be too precise or scientific about birds and trees and flowers . . . a certain free margin, and even vagueness—perhaps ignorance, credulity—helps your enjoyment of these things."
Walt Whitman

March's warmth brings both long-awaited color to tree limbs and the springtime song of birds to our gardens.

EVERGREEN
FENCES

~

I was a woefully terrible science student. These days I read in the newspaper and hear on TV that this is because when I was coming along, girls were told they *couldn't* do well in science. I never remember anyone telling me I couldn't do well in science. Quite to the contrary, everyone told me I *could* do well.

At home, my father was an engineer—a mechanical engineer at that. Not only could he figure everything out, he could fix it as well. He told me I could do anything I wanted to.

At school, by junior high, most of the science teachers were men. To my impressionable, very feminine adolescent mind, these learned men were my heroes. One, Mr. Vought, a young teacher just out of college, was adorable as well as learned. None of them ever told me I couldn't do well. They encouraged me to do better.

Furthermore, back then, once you passed the required general science and biology classes no more science was required. But the elective sciences—chemisty and physics—were the classes where the boys were, and, of course, one boy in particular. I *had* to take them! To impress him I toiled and struggled, pretending to be interested in things I neither understood nor had the slightest natural talent for.

For him I endured the smell of wretched formulas bubbling over Bun-sen burners. For him I stayed up till the dawn hours memorizing the formula that would measure how much water is displaced by a solid mass ($w=mg$). Actually, memorizing it was the easy part. The impossible part was learning how to make the wretched formula work. To this day I remember the knot in my stomach when the test was handed back and, peeping inside my lengthwise-folded paper, instead of a grade, I saw "See me" discreetly written in red pencil. Wisely I dropped physics and took world history. Everything in that class came so easily that I wondered if I might have lived through those times so long ago.

What, you must be wondering, has any of this to do with gardens? More than you might imagine—for my one and only shining moment in any science class is a moment I owe to my mother's constant observations about flowers, trees, and birds.

It was a Saturday afternoon. I was five or six. We were on our customary drive home from the in-town grocery store to our outskirts-of-town home in Moore Country, North Carolina.

That particular afternoon, as we drove down the familiar stretch of road bordered by farmlands and fields, I remember that Mother began pointing out how the cows were grazing in pastureland marked by wire-and-pole fences near the rustic red barns built close to the farmhouses. Then she remarked about how you don't see the barbed wire or the poles made from whittled-down tree trunks that separate one man's land from

"I think

that

I shall

never see

A poem as

lovely as

a tree."

~

Joyce Kilmer

his neighbors' land. What you *do* see outlining each farm's boundary are tall, majestic evergreen trees. I still remember taking a long look at that stand of trees—their limbs weaving a lush screen of slender long pine needles tangled around bushy cedar branches, their various shades of greens braided in and around one another. How different they looked from the scruffy bushes that grew close to the road.

"Do you know how those trees got there?" Mother asked in her matter-of-fact schoolteacher voice as she pointed to the perfectly peaked fir trees.

"I guess somebody planted them," I surely replied, though I don't remember my answer. But I do remember how she answered her own question. It was something like this.

"Little birds pluck the seeds out from the pinecones in the trees in the woods for their dinner. Then those same little birds sit on the farmer's fence and sing and sing and sing, their tummies full. Sometimes when a little bird opens his mouth to sing, he drops a seed he was saving for dessert. Other times, a tiny seed will pass through the bird's body undigested and plop down on the ground. Then the rich soil and the warm sun and the gentle rain come along and nourish the seed. Soon a baby tree comes up and eventually it grows into a proud tree."

I'm sure I never gave this homespun elementary science lesson another thought until one day in Miss Lucy Stone's fourth-grade class.

"Does anyone know how the rows of trees along the highway fences get there?" she asked in her always-prim manner.

I waved my hand so frantically she had to call on me. When she did, I blurted out the story Mother had told me in my grown-up fourth-grade language. "Birds sit on the fence and drop seeds on the ground."

I got an A in science that day.

Who would imagine that tiny birds planted this dense evergreen fence over the many years ?

TOR GARDEN

~

"The garden of the world is California," Belle Angier wrote in 1906. Seeing California's gardens for the first time is a breathtaking experience. You expect to be astonished by the giant redwoods and fragrant avenues lined with stately eucalyptus trees. But the camellias are twice the size of those in Louisiana and South Carolina. The December roses put to shame those that bloom in May and June on the East Coast. And despite the overcrowded and smoggy conditions in once-untouched open fields and meadows, wild flowers are everywhere, especially golden sun-kissed poppies.

California has many grand and glamorous gardens. There is Filoli with its Chartres Cathedral window garden, San Francisco's Japanese Tea Garden with its precisely placed walks and bridges, the Moorteen Botanical Gardens with their spectacular display of desert plants, and, of course, Huntington Gardens with their magnificent formal statuary and over 9,000 varieties of plants. Yet my own favorite garden is a small place

Even in the California mist, before the sun breaks through, bright vibrant colors in the dooryard garden warm the somber gray rocks of Tor House (above and opposite, top).

tucked away on a winding, twisting street in the picture-perfect town of Carmel-by-the-Sea. It is the garden at Tor House, the home of the American poet Robinson Jeffers. My friend George Thornally knew I would love Tor House when he first took me there many years ago.

Like most people, at first glance I was struck by the uniqueness of the house that Jeffers himself had hand-built. Red stones from the Great Wall of China, pebbles from Tintagel Castle (the legendary home of King Arthur), a piece from the pyramid of Cheops, chips of marble gathered after the great San Francisco earthquake, even Native American arrowheads are embedded among the enormous rocks hauled from the beach below to build the house, its nearby freestanding castlelike structure, Hawk Tower, the garden walks, and surrounding walls. Now that I have been there many times, I find it is the garden more than the house that remains ever awe-inspiring. For Tor garden, more than any other garden I know, is a canvas of nature's contrasts painted against a background of breaking ocean waves and boundless sky.

My most recent visit there was on a gray day, of which there are many in Carmel—days as gray as the enormous stones of Tor House. Nevertheless the green lawn was lush, the flowers lustrously bright. Their rich and varied colors, brilliant enough to dazzle the eye, were made even brighter by the drabness of the centuries-old rocks and overcast sky. Each bloom's delicate fragility

*V*ines covered in tiny crepe-paper blossoms resembling wild roses (left) creep around rough seashells that have been carefully placed along the garden's edge.

A great dawn-color rose widening the petals around her gold eye peers day and night in the window," Jeffers wrote describing a rose in his garden. Might this be the rose, I wondered, remembering the vibrant colors I have seen in the breaking dawn on other days.

became all the more remarkable as the flowers swayed in the wind, brushing against cragged walls impervious to the elements.

Flush with these observations, I glimpsed a perfectly formed blossom that somehow had crept up through a tiny crack, truly no wider than a butterfly's wing, in the stone walkway. I was spellbound. How did it get there? Why had it not been trampled to death?

As George and I walked along the pathway, we came to the stone wall and gate that mark the drop from the garden to the beach and ocean below. There, where the sky meets the wall, a rose bush, heavy with full-blown deep-coral blossoms, reached skyward. The beauty of the scene and the poignancy of the image moved me deeply. Some feelings are too personal to share even with close friends. In silence we strolled back to the car.

Months later, back in my North Carolina home some three thousand miles away from Carmel, I read Robinson Jeffers's poem, "Shears," and I remembered Tor garden, its roses, and that insightful moment.

A great dawn-color rose widening the
  petals around her gold eye
Peers day and night in the window. She
  watches us
Breakfasting, lighting lamps, reading,
  and the children playing, and the
  dogs by the fire,
She watches earnestly, uncomprehending,
As we stare into the world of trees and
  roses uncomprehending,

There is a great gulf fixed. But even while
  I gaze, and the rose at me, my little
  flower-greedy daughter-in-law
Walks with shears, very blonde and
  housewifely
Through the small garden, and
  suddenly the rose finds herself
  rootless in-doors.
Now she is part of the life she watched.
—So we: death comes and plucks us:
  we become part of the living earth
And wind and water whom we so loved.
  We are they.

*I*t is little wonder that through the ages poets continue to extol the beauty and mystery of the rose.

"Bitter are the tears of a child: Sweeten them.

Deep are the thoughts of a child: Quiet them.

Sharp is the grief of a child: Take it from him.

Soft is the heart of a child: Do not harden it."

"A Child,"

Lady Pamela Wyndham Glenconner

THE HEART
OF A CHILD

*J*t didn't take a second look to know the squiggly blue lines on the rough gray sidewalk were a child's hopscotch game. Nor did it take a second thought to know what was going on in the mind of the little girl who had drawn them. There she sat in the fading late afternoon light, scrunched over on the steep steps leading from the sidewalk up to the front

ran to a cluster of budding daffodils, and picked the only one that had dared to bloom that unseasonably warm Valentine's Day.

"Coming," she called, skipping toward the front door, taking a little bit of the outdoors inside with her.

Have there ever been more dreaded words to the contented outdoors child than "It's time to come in"? Who wants to go in when there are so many wonders in the yard? There are trees to climb, dark bushes to hide in, leaves to kick around, pebbles to toss, squirrels to chase, flowers to sniff, buttercups and daisies to rope together, berries to gather, and best of all, clouds to drift away on and stars to wish upon.

Those who think a garden is a playground for a child's body are only partly right. The garden is also the playground for the child's mind, for the spirit.

And if there is a happier joy for an adult than watching a playful young child in the garden, I don't know what it is. Yet not everyone shares that sentiment.

"Children pick the flowers!" grumpy voices complain.

I never worry about picked flowers. We adults don't pick enough flowers. We leave them to fade on their stems, keeping new growth and fresh blossoms from beginning.

"Why, they trample the flowers!" cantankerous disbelievers protest.

What damage can small feet possibly do? Little footprints are only reminders of visitors who couldn't resist getting closer, and they certainly aren't as harm-

*W*ho needs a pebble or broken piece of glass for hopscotch when nature has provided a profusion of camellia blossoms dropped from a nearby shrub?

door. She was trying her best to hide.

"It's time to come in," her mother pleaded from the front door. It was clearly not her mother's first request.

Of course I did not intend to intrude. I was just taking a walk. But there I was, and she had been seen.

She cast a disgusted look my way. Full of bad temper, she stomped up the steps. Suddenly she broke her stride,

ful as heavy fallen branches or a free-roaming dog with an uncontrollable urge to dig.

I know of no better place than the garden filled with sunshine, warmth, beauty, and color for even the youngest child to learn about life. When children are quiet and take the time to watch the birds, the plants, the sky, they begin to learn values that will stay with them always.

My own children couldn't have been more than four and six when a mother and father wren began building a nest in a hollow column by their grandparents' back door. We had hours of fun watching those industrious little birds carrying bits of string and straw, twigs and grass. They worked from sunup to sundown until their home was ready, then things settled down for a few days. We knew the morning the babies hatched because the mother no longer left the nest. Rather, she kept a watchful eye, while the father flew back and forth, back and forth, back and forth, bringing bugs and insects so small we could hardly see them in his beak.

Langdon and Joslin were thrilled that special day when the baby birds poked their heads above the rim of the column to see the world that awaited them. That was the same day a neighbor's cat caught a robin and left only a few feathers as evidence of his delectable dinner strewn across the adjoining yards. Of course the children were terribly worried that the little wrens would meet the same horrible fate. How relieved we all were only a

few days later when, as the mother bird watched, each little bird, after taking a few hops along the nearby column ledge, tenuously flew to the nearest tree branch, rested, and then flew safely away. From that time on, a family of wrens adopted the grannies' house every spring.

One year, though, tragedy struck. We happened to be visiting in Danville that Sunday. Langdon heard the wild flurry of chirping first. Soon we all did. "Get the broom!" my husband Clauston shouted. "Get in the house!" I shrieked.

While Joslin and I watched from inside, somehow Langdon and Clauston got the monstrous (to me, at least,) slithering black snake off the column. But it was too late. He had already devoured the eggs. "We'll never have the little wrens again," we said sadly. Yet the next year they did come back.

How many insights the children received from our feathered friends. They learned that daily tasks must go on in the

Children see wondrous things we adults walk right past. If William hadn't calmly and innocently asked, "Emyl, did you ever see a turtle in the garden before?" I would have moved on to the next spectacular array of flowers at Monticello. Instead we all crowded around as quiet as the field mice and waited, and waited, until he stuck his head all the way out for us, and the crowd that had gathered to admire.

Unusual trees and flowers stretch every child's imagination, from the gentle powder puff-like blossoms of the mimosa tree (above) to the exotic plumage of the Bird of Paradise (above right).

dark of rain and the joy of the sun—and tasks must be shared. They saw how, despite impending dangers and the threat of the unknown, nature's creatures build for the future. They found out that their worst fears may never develop. They experienced the heartbreak we feel when grief comes unexpectedly. And they learned the delight of surprise.

I often think back to those simple lessons these days as mind-boggling global and technological changes relentlessly press down around us. I watch worried people leading complicated lives seeking convoluted and complex answers to their problems. If only they could spend a few peaceful hours in the garden with the eyes of a child.

In the garden, life's problems are swept away by an ethereal magic that all can feel and understand. Take the time, alone and in silence, to let these thoughts drift over you. Then share them with the children. For those who learn to love the garden will learn to love life.

"As the Rose-tree is composed of the sweetest Flowers and the sharpest Thorns; as the heavens are sometimes fair and sometimes overcast, alternately tempestuous and serene; so is the Life of Man intermingled with Hopes and Fears, with Joys and Sorrows, with Pleasures and with Pains."

Robert Burton

A HIDING PLACE

"I see the garden thicket's shade
Where all the summer long we played,
And gardens set and houses made . . ."

Mary Howitt

"Where did you used to hide in the garden?" the somewhat formidable and sophisticated curator asked me as we turned the bend in the path and came upon a canopy of wisteria twined above a thick, low-growing hedge. How we adults love to share the playful games and pleasures that we, like children from time immemorial, long ago enjoyed in the garden!

I was luckier than most city children. Next to our house there was a vacant lot. Before they built a house on it, it was filled with wiry shrubs, unpruned trees, thick, tangled thickets, even gnarled honeysuckle vines—a perfect secret garden home.

The question raised, my scholarly friend and I put aside our more intellectual discussions and whiled away the afternoon exchanging tales of running away, or just slipping away, to our secret hiding places. Later, I mailed him this enchanting passage written in the 1920s by Eleanor Gordon Parker that tells of her exceptionally beautiful and private garden home:

I was impatient for my sister to be old enough to play in the garden with me. When at last she was permitted to do so, I was wild with delight. How we loved that garden with its violet-bordered paths, its pink azaleas, its snowdrops, its coral and white and pale pink camellias, its violets and its century plants. And how we delighted in the yucca trees and the fig tree and the pomegranate tree and the screen of bamboo trees at the back. One tree, whose name fails me, gave us each a private apartment among its leaves, with a drawing room in which a thick branch was our davenport and a slender branch our piano. I seem to remember this tree as always green, and when it was in flower its small white blossoms were spicy and fragrant.

Anyone who has hidden among the branches of shrubs and trees knows you are never alone in your special place, no matter how well hidden it is. Woodland and garden spirits hide there, too, as well as baby birds, chipmunks, and squirrels. That's why to this day I never pass the ancient oak tree at the foot of our street without glancing over and wondering about the invisible, but very real, tiny folk who live in the hollowed-out covey.

PLANTING THE CHILD'S GARDEN

"There was

a pretty

dandelion

With lovely,

fluffy hair,

That glis-

tened in the

sunshine

And in the

summer air.

But oh!

this pretty

dandelion

Soon grew

old and grey;

And, sad

to tell! her

charming

hair

Blew many

miles away."

Anonymous

What child of any age can resist reaching out to finger a blooming flower, ripening vegetable, or leaves on a tree branch? From a tiny tot in a stroller to a melancholy teenager on a lonely walk, young people revel in the magic of the garden. Though many parks, gardens, and conservatories feature children's areas, the best child's garden of all is the one in his or her own yard where nature's ever changing wonders unfold firsthand, day by day.

To experience the garden at any age, but especially as a child, is to explore myriad senses and emotions. To smell the delicate cotton-candy fragrance of airy pinks, to taste the sweetness of a sun-warmed strawberry, to laugh at oversized green elephant ears flopping in the summer breezes, to thrill at the touch of the velvety lamb's ear, to hear the deep buzz of a bee busily darting from one cone flower to the next is truly to embrace the marvels of life.

In the garden a child's imagination knows no bounds. Friends can play hide-and-seek, climb on tree limbs, and skip and dance with abandon—all the while pretending to be anyone, from a daring cowboy to a graceful ballerina. And the garden provides a secret meeting place for the child's special friends—those imaginary playmates unseen to anyone but the child. (Like many only children, I had a pair of twin friends who lived in my garden, Palmy and Malmy.)

THE LITTLE SWITCHES

To hear her mother tell it, my cousin, Susan Buckingham, was not always the perfect little lady. She was petite, quiet-spoken, and polite—but that was out in public, and everyone knows children will be children. At home, it seems, Susan was known to have a rambunctious side.

The family story goes that one week usually mischievous Susan was truly as good as gold. Her mother couldn't help noticing her daughter's exemplary behavior, but rather than wonder what had brought it about, she simply enjoyed the peaceful, blissful days. The reason for Susan's demeanor was discovered one morning when the little girl took her mother by the hand, and led her to the living room, straight to the flower vase filled with spring's first forsythia boughs that had been brought inside to force the tight buds open. "Look, Mommy," Susan exclaimed, pointing to the star-shaped yellow blossoms, "the little switches bloomed!"

Each year when the forsythia boughs are full of plump bulging buds just waiting to catch enough sun to burst open in yellow splendor, I clip a few, take them inside, put "Susan," my little stone garden ornament, by the vase, and together we wait for the little switches to bloom.

But how do you know when the forsythia is ripe for the picking? No one says it better than did Beverly Nichols in 1932 in *Down the Garden Path*.

If you go out and run your fingers over the shrub, you will find quantities of young branches bearing an abundance of buds. Some of these buds may be barely formed; they may show you only a gleam of yellow with a reddish-brown tip; they may be cluttered up with a lot of dead wood. Be brave! Slice off those branches. Carry them indoors. Trim off the dead wood. Place the result in water. Leave it for a week in a dark, warm cupboard. When you return you will find … a bright, sturdy array of blossom that lasts, literally for weeks. Then, as you tuck some asparagus fern into the vase and transport it proudly to your desk, you will feel inclined to ask the question, "Who said that it was cruel to cut flowers, when these are as happy as primroses in a sheltered corner?" And, one might add, as expensive looking as any spray of orchids.

To a child a garden is, one minute, a sunny fairyland, all blue and pink. The next minute it is a sinister place, a lagoon or cave filled with dragons and dark, ugly creatures. The garden truly is a miniature wonderland with no boundaries or limits—and it lives with you throughout your adult life.

"Did you ever trap a bumblebee in a foxglove blossom so you could hear it buzz louder and louder, all the time hoping you wouldn't get stung?" a tourist asked me in the garden of the Old Stone House as I dodged a perturbed bee.

"When I was a little girl and wanted to pretend I was grown up enough to wear makeup I would pick the fluffy soft mimosa blossoms off the trees and

A stately foxglove becomes a playful toy to a child's mind.

den fence. "I know just the ivory yellow color a blossom has to be for the nectar to be the sweetest."

Children should have their own garden plot to tend and watch, to learn from, and to play in. A child's garden should be a carefree place—not one with a plotted scheme or faultless design. A child's garden should be a grand mixture of flowers and plants that children can identify through their books, songs, and rhymes. If your own garden is a perfectly manicured showcase, plant your children's patchwork garden in another part of the yard! Make it their own little special nook.

Plant the most colorful, fragrant, and varied textured plants you can find in your child's garden. Take a moment to think back to your own childhood and the flowers and vegetables you loved the most. There must be daisies to pluck the petals from, one by one, and to string into a daisy-chain necklace. There should be a few tulips to tiptoe through and to use as imaginary goblets. And even the smallest garden has room for a cherry tomato plant or two—just the right size for little fingers and mouths. And, if you have the space, don't forget the green bean vines for Jack to climb.

pretend they were powder puffs," the kindly grandmother told her grandchildren in the garden at Monticello.

"I still can't pass up a honeysuckle vine in an old-fashioned garden," a rather stuffy friend surprised me by saying one summer's day as he picked a bunch of honeysuckle blossoms from my gar-

Every little girl should have a blue forget-me-not plant in her garden. No other miniature flower is so absolutely perfect for a doll or fairy bouquet. And little boys of every generation are fascinated by the snapping jaws of the snapdragon. Fast-germinating seeds, marigolds and zinnias, for example, are especially fascinating to watch. And don't overlook herbs. Just a few sprigs of mint, lamb's ear, lemon balm, and catnip offer a wonderful variety of textures, colors, and fragrances.

Most important, let the children make some of the selections themselves and help them learn about different flowers and vegetables by explaining their unique characteristics. Give your children their own set of small gardening tools just the right size for their little hands, including that childhood favorite—the brightly painted watering can. Even beach pails and shovels, little wagons, and wheelbarrows can be useful "working toys" for gardening duties.

In many towns there are junior gardening clubs or special summertime gardening activities for children of all ages; some recreational departments and natural history museums also sponsor children's gardening programs. The Park Seed Company (see Directory) has a special Children's Choice Seed Collection and a national garden contest.

Remember, too, that the child's garden holds untold opportunities for learning experiences other than growing and harvesting flowers, herbs, and vegetables. What better place could there be for reading the myriad children's books and tales set out of doors, or for drawing and painting, learning about colors, light, and shadow, and making observations? There is no better place to just be together. In an unfettered, peaceful garden your children will learn to love art, to love nature, and to love one another.

A Gift from the Garden
MR. AND MRS. EGG HEAD

Children are so curious to learn about nature. A delightful planting project that has echoed down through the years is Mr. and Mrs. Egg Head. Granted, I never thought about planting grass seed in an eggshell, painting a face on it, and naming it when I was a child. But when chatting about our grandmothers' gardens the other day, my friend Louise Talley and I recalled how we used to watch tender flower seedlings sprout up in eggshells placed on a warm, sunny window before they were planted outside.

Here are my assistant Liza's instructions for making Mr. and Mrs. Egg Heads with your children or grandchildren:

Help your child poke a small hole in the small end of a raw egg with a straight pin, then enlarge it with fingernail scissors to about a half inch in diameter. Puncture the inner sac, turn the egg upside down, and gently shake out the insides. (Mothers, be sure to make several batches of chocolate chip cookies with the eggs!) When the eggshell is empty, gently fill it with potting soil and sprinkle a few seeds of rye grass seed on top. Wet this down. Set the eggs in a sunny spot, either inside your house or out, and water lightly each day. With a little love and care, your eggheads will soon have full heads of hair. Once the grass has sprouted, use colorful felt-tip pens to draw egg-head eyes, noses, and mouths. Be sure to give them names!

Fences to climb and playhouses for tea. To my way of thinking, gardens should be for children first.

From ghosty-ghoulies and whimsical fairy chairs to story-book garden friends, the yard is a backdrop for any variety of moods and scenes.

GOURDS

~

Sugar in the gourd and honey in the horn,
I never was so happy since the hour I was born.

As a third-grader I sang those silly lines from "Turkey in the Straw." The words we recited by rote meant nothing to us but our minds have a way of holding on to lines of poetry and verses of songs we learned in our childhood. Years later, always to our astonishment, when something jogs our memory, the words tumble out of our lips.

Thank goodness no one was with me the day I passed the gourd farm on a little-traveled back road in Saluda County, South Carolina. Otherwise they would have had to listen to me first hum and then sing that silly song. It came back to me as I rounded a curve. There, next to the Carolina red-mud field where they had once grown on thin, sprawling vines, long-throated speckled gourds were piled high, ready for the choosing. Most were priced 25 and 50 cents, but those with the hole for a family of nesting birds already bored were $1.00.

"Sugar in the gourd?" If only I had been born a century earlier, I would have known the meaning of the line. Back then gourds were used for countless purposes around the house and the yard. In the old days not just sugar, but lard and other staples were stored in hollowed-out gourds on the back porch and in the cold storage cellar. Fully scooped-out gourds were perfect ladles for drawing water from a well bucket or a clear spring.

To keep an ample supply of gourds on hand, vines were planted on fences around country homes. In fact they were advertised in Childs's 1898 spring seed catalog as bearing fantastic and grotesque fruit and being suitable for "covering sheds, training over fences or brush piles, and always sure to attract the attention of the children, who love to play with the pretty striped and oddly crooked fruits."

Those were the same days when little boys, Huck Finn-style, carried their fishing bait—snails, worms, and maggots—in gourds tied to the end of their homemade fishing poles. And when a family moved away from a house, leaving it untended and uninhabited, the old saying was, "Kill the cats and burn the fat gourds." A hundred years ago gourds were so much a part of a country household's function, that when the cats and gourds were gone, nothing was left.

These days gourds are mostly decorative. In Waco, Kentucky, Donna Smith uses locally grown gourds as canvases for painting her colorful Christmas scenes. Seeing the gourd's everlasting charm and many possible uses, you may be tempted to plant a vine or two yourself if you have the space.

"The loft follower of the sun, Sad when he sets, shuts up her yellow leaves, Drooping all night, and when he warm returns, Points her enamored bosom to his ray."

James Thomson

What child or adult cannot help but be charmed by the pansies' playful little faces?

"You must wake and call me early,
*   call me early, mother dear;*
Tomorrow 'ill be the happiest time
*   of all the glad New Year . . .*
For I'm to be Queen o' the May, mother,
*   I'm to be Queen of the May."*

"The May Queen,"
Alfred, Lord Tennyson

MAY DAY

My bedroom in the modest Moore County, North Carolina, clapboard house we lived in when I was five years old wasn't very large. The only furnishings I distinctly remember are my bed and a white painted chest. I haven't the vaguest idea what color the walls were or where my toys were kept. I do remember the floor and the ceiling, though. They were huge.

On the floor, in the center of the room, was a large, square, black-bordered linoleum rug. Within its patterns lived every friend any child would ever want to have. Jack and Jill, Mistress Mary, and Little Boy Blue played on the hills and in the dales. Best of all, my nursery-rhyme friends, unlike real people, young and old, were always there.

They were there when I crawled out of bed, early or late, each morning. They were there on sweltering August days when it was no fun to play outside and February days when it rained instead of snowing. They were there when the children who lived close by had better things to do than to play with me. They were there when Mother and Daddy went out, leaving me with a babysitter. But most important of all, they were there when I crept into bed each night.

Does anyone see a host of umbrella-capped toadstools and not look closer for woodland spirits?

Bedtime was something of a ritual. First the shades were drawn. Always my prayers were said with my eyes squeezed shut, but not so tight I couldn't steal one last glance at my make-believe friends to make sure all was right in their world, as well as mine. Then, when I was well tucked in, the covers pulled high under my chin, I'd squeeze my eyes really tight and listen for Mother or Daddy to click out the overhead light.

The tighter I squeezed them the blacker the darkened room would become. Quietly and slowly I counted. One ... two ... three ... four .... until, at just the right moment, I would blink my eyes wide open.

There, on the ceiling of my room, my own private heaven of silvery stars twinkled brightly above me. Daddy had seen the glow-in-the-dark stars advertised in a catalog and ordered them for me. Against Mother's protests, he had pasted them all across my ceiling. Every night I drifted off gazing up at a wonderland of stars, singing to myself, Twinkle, twinkle little star, how I wonder what you are, up above the world so high, like a diamond in the sky.

I was a dreamy sort of girl back in 1946, years before TV came to rural North Carolina. I had yet to see the dancing flowers of *Fantasia*, in Technicolor, no less. But in my room, meadows of exquisite flowers bloomed year-round on flawless green hills under an always watchful, cloudless, starlit sky.

Outside, gossamer fairies pirouetted through pink clover beds, sipped honeysuckle tea from rose petals beneath ruffled toadstools while dressed in their finest hollyhock frocks and buttercup hats, and rode on the Queen Butterfly's wings from flower to flower. I had seen them. Others had too. I had proof. There were pictures of them, just like the ones

I had seen in the pages of my two favorite books, *Story-a-Day* and *Andersen's Fairy Tales*.

The fairies lived in my mother's springtime garden. Fairies were gentle and kind, the bringers of beauty. With a wave of their wands, tight, colorless flower buds opened to a rainbow of pinks, yellows, lilacs, and pale blues, just like the colors in my big crayon box.

There has never been a more beautiful spring than that spring— at least in my mind. Fairy rings were everywhere in the lawn. The velvety moss was never greener or softer. Butterfly chariots darted among the flowers all day long. My heart was filled with springtime dreams. That year, more than anything else I dreamed of having a May basket filled with yellow-eyed white daisies, graceful, petticoatlike poppies, and silky pink roses. At the handle of my basket there would be a profusion of long curlicue pink and blue ribbons.

I can still see the streams of the spring morning sun throwing bright silver beams on my windowsill the first day of May the year I was five. I can still smell the sweet bouquet of spring wafting through my slightly open bedroom window. I can still remember slipping out the back door around to the front of the house to see if a May basket was waiting at my front door. My heart fell when I spied the lonesome gray front porch, spanking clean, but as empty as it could be.

Well, I would certainly have to do something about that. Barefoot and still

in my nightgown, I bounded through the dewy grass to the flower border that ran along our side yard. I gathered a handful of spring flowers, blue and pink. I didn't know all their names then. Today I imagine they were dianthus, violets, phlox, and maybe a few late-blooming bluebells.

Clutching the flowers, I quietly

The eternal charm of spring flowers reminds us of May's gentle days.

Though the centuries-old traditions of daisy chains and Maypoles remain part of springtime celebrations at Meredith (below right and opposite top) and Saint Mary's (opposite bottom) colleges in Raleigh, North Carolina, in many other schools like my own college, Mary Washington in Fredericksburg, Virginia (which is now coed), those days must be relived in old black-and white photographs. Far left and above left is Jamie Redwood, the 1941 Mary Washington College May Queen.

A Gift from the Garden
CHILDREN'S HERBAL TEA

Long ago when the English discovered that their tea, made delicious by adding several lumps of sugar, was giving children cavities, they concocted a special tea just for the children. By using a blend of dried fruits and flowers they made a tea so sweet even the children didn't ask for sugar. Today you can buy an already blended children's tea, or you can make your own by combining your and, of course, your children's favorite dried fruits and flowers and brewing it the way you would any loose tea.

Bob Johnson, whose Raleigh, North Carolina, shop, Cameron Park Botanicals, is an herb lover's Eden, suggests mixing equal amounts of dried apples, lemon peels and orange peels to which you add a generous helping of dried lavender flowers and rosehips. You will need only a small amount of each ingredient to make enough tea to last for a week or so. Begin with two or three slices of the apple, lemon, and orange peels. Chop finely either in the food processor or by hand. Stir in a teaspoon or more of the sweet dried herbs also chopped into little pieces. The grand thing about making this tea is that you can add additional portions of specific ingredients until you get just the flavor you like. The mixture is wonderfully colorful, the tea brews up to a rosy red, and the taste and aroma you won't believe! It is almost like drinking liquid cotton candy!

English children call this special tea "blue eyes," but its soft pink color after brewing is more reminiscent of rosy cheeks.

slipped back into the house, tiptoed through the kitchen, and then burst into the dining room. I knew I'd find Mother there having her morning coffee. "Happy May Day!" I squealed.

Many years later, one May when I was arranging flowers in a basket I asked Mother if she ever had any idea how much I wanted a May basket when I was a little girl. She never had any inkling of my dream of dreams. But she had, unknowingly, at least partially fulfilled my secret longings. In those days "May Day" was a special celebration at the women's schools, seminaries, and colleges of which there were so many. These days, sadly, those schools are mostly closed or have gone coed. That year, on the first Saturday in May we drove to Raleigh to see my grandparents and go to May Day at Saint Mary's. Later, when we moved to Danville, each year we would attend *two* college May Days on two different spring Saturdays—one at Stratford and one at Averett. There, on the gently rolling college campuses dressed in full spring beauty, I saw the "big girls," some in long flowing white dresses, others costumed in medieval English garb, dance and sing, scattering rose petals on the lawn and dancing around the Maypole— a magical sight to any "little girl."

Many years later, thirty-plus years in fact, I was thrilled when my daughter, Joslin, brought a flower-decorated, crayoned note home announcing that her kindergarten group at Storybook Farm would celebrate May Day that year. I'm quite sure I loved her flower-banded

To celebrate its sesquicentennial in April, 1992, Saint Mary's College chose the Maypole theme. What could be lovelier or more colorful?

*E*veryone enjoys a flower-filled basket. Why not be creative and turn an inexpensive straw hat into a floral centerpiece?

picture hat and her long, flaring, frilly-skirted dress much more than she did. That was one of her tomboy years when, to her way of thinking, tree limbs were made to swing *from* rather than to hold swings. But she wore the dress and hat and carried a May basket anyway and I loved every minute of it. Which is why, one beautiful May day last year for no reason at all I set up a table in the yard, brought out my children's collection of Beatrix Potter figurines, and invited Sarah, Chip's four-year-old daughter, and her friend, Jackie, over for a surprise ice-cream party. Oh, I told them the party was for them, but it was really for me.

That night, just as I was drifting off to sleep, I squeezed my eyes really tight and then opened them for just a moment. In that half a second I saw a thousand twinkling stars dancing on my bedroom ceiling and my heart soared.

⌒

"I never wander 'mong the flowers,
But mem'ry will be straying
To other days and other hours,
When childhood went a May-ing.

O precious days, O happy hours,
How mem'ry backward lingers,
To pluck again the dewy flowers,
With childhood's rosy fingers.

O give me back that olden time,
When childhood knew no sorrow;
But only cared to pluck life's flowers,
And dreamed not of the morrow."

Anonymous

A *Gift from the Garden*
SURPRISE FLOWERPOT DESSERT

A delightful garden party dessert that will delight big as well as little girls is this quick and easy version of the painstaking and hard-to-make baked Alaska. To make eight servings you will need eight 3-inch-diameter terra-cotta flowerpots, 1/2 gallon of any flavor ice cream (for a real treat use the Cookies and Cream, Chocolate Chip, or Rocky Road flavor), a ten ounce tub of Cool Whip, and one package of Oreos. Begin by softening the ice cream. Set aside eight Oreo cookies and place one in the bottom of each flowerpot to cover the drainage hole. Crush the remaining cookies until they resemble rich potting soil. Beginning with the ice cream, spread alternating layers of ice cream, Cool Whip, and Oreo crumbs, ending with a thick topping of the cookie crumbs. Place the pots in the freezer until serving time. Garnish with a few fresh garden flowers and if you're in a playful mood, add a gummy worm!

MORE THAN JUST A BOWL

𝓤nlike Edna St. Vincent Millay, I never could resist plucking a handful of windblown daffodils or gathering a bunch of chubby-cheeked purple pansies, either as a little girl, or now.

These days I pick flowers not just in my garden but also from the street vendor's canopied stall, and out of the strategically placed white plastic buckets at my neighborhood grocery store. It would be terrible to leave those fragile blossoms cramped together in rubber-band-fastened cellophane wrappers to wither and fade under those harsh fluorescent lights. And so, every week, even when my own garden is overflowing with anemone and roses, irises and candytuft, I rescue a handful of hothouse-grown pink carnations, baby's breath, and

Attics, basements, even pantries yield unlimited possibilities to hold your favorite flowers.

purplish-blue statice and take them home along with my English muffins, turkey breast, and cat food.

And, every week, once I've gotten them home, I face the same dilemma— one you're undoubtedly familiar with. That's why this chapter is dedicated to everyone who has ever grown, or received as a gift, a beautiful bouquet of blossoms, only to despair, "*What* am I going to do with them? What am I going to *put* them in?!"

My answer is, "Put them in anything,

except those ugly, pebbly, green containers and those bland sandy-beige baskets the florists buy by the gross." Go up into your attic, or down into your basement, or to the back of your catch-everything closet and you'll find something to put them in. I guarantee it.

Every home has scores of unused, dusty, often forgotten treasures—from the eggshell-thin antique demitasse cup that long ago lost its saucer, to the marigold Carnival glass bowl that hasn't seen the light of day since you packed it away, keeping it only because it belonged to your grandmother. Take them out. Fill them with a few sprightly Johnny-jump-ups or a ravishing bounty of exotic orchids. Before your eyes, like ugly ducklings transformed into graceful swans, those castoffs will become beautiful showpieces. Flowers enhance the objects that hold them.

When displayed well, each bowl, vase, goblet, or curious little container takes on a personality all its own. Each inanimate object can become perfect— unique, charming, even whimsical. And each one holds memories and special thoughts we can enjoy the same way we delight in the beauty, the textures, and the fragrance of the flowers in them.

For years, a pair of lovely white-and-gold flowered Victorian vases sat on opposite ends of the mantel in my parents' living room. Mother told me umpteen times that these very vases had once been proudly displayed on the mantel in my New England grandparents' home. Oddly enough, I never remember seeing flowers in these vases in our home, and I don't know if my grandmother ever used them for flowers. But this I do remember: When Christmas and other special days that called for flowers on the mantel came around, Mother carefully took the vases down. She ceremoniously placed them high on the top shelf of the New England secretary-bookcase for safekeeping behind the locked, gleaming cherry panel doors.

Now that the vases are in my own home, my habits are the exact opposite of my mother's. On most days of the year the vases are safe on one of the upper shelves of the bookcases in the den. Then, on special occasions, I painstakingly take them down, fill them with flowers, and place them on my living room mantel for all to enjoy.

These vases, so special to me now, were the rage in the Victorian homes of the 1850s—and mine show their age. Many people really do not care how old their vases are. But they do want them to be in perfect condition. To me, the scuffs and scratches, even the little nicks on the flower petals and flaking gilt paint become lovely reminders of other hands in another time that also delighted in their loveliness.

Mother remembered only seeing these vases in my grandparents' home. I think, though, because they date from the nineteenth century, they must have belonged to my great-grandparents. Actually, with the simple white background and gold-tipped flowers, my vases are rather plain examples. Wealthier people,

or those who preferred a fancier style, had more elaborately decorated vases— ones with deep magenta or cobalt blue backgrounds and glorious sprays of multicolored flowers. Plain or fancy, this style of vase was trumpet-shaped with a wide, flaring mouth just right for a large spray of flowers and greenery reminiscent of a Victorian garden.

That's why I find my mantel to be its prettiest when these delicate vases are

I never knew my great-grandparents, who first owned this flower-encrusted vase, but when it is filled with spring flowers I think of how they must have enjoyed them.

*W*hile others prefer dramatic, well thought-through arrange-ments, my preference is for a few flowers lovingly placed in whatever container suits my mood or captures my fancy at the moment.

$\mathscr{S}$ilver baskets, goblets, even a sterling salt shaker that long ago lost its top, are perfect for my dressing table and more formal rooms, but I would never give up my pottery pieces or simple little china and glass vases. To me each container holds memories as well as flowers.

filled to overflowing with old-fashioned yellow roses, pink Gerber daisies, blue irises, spidery Queen Anne's lace, delicate larkspur, and trailing English ivy. Even when they are empty and "put up" for safekeeping, I never think of them merely as white vases. They are favorite family pieces patiently waiting for an excuse to be taken down, dusted off, and used once again.

Just as loved as that pair of vases is a single miniature vase. It must have been my grandmother's when she was a little girl for I found it in her domed-top leather trunk among her precious childhood possessions—a hand-stitched Little Red Riding Hood rag doll, pieces of her dolls' teaset, and a bulging scrapbook filled with lace-bordered valentines and silk bookmarks painted with lovely, sentimental sayings. How thrilled I was that the barely one-inch-tall vase is still in remarkably good condition.

Now, every May I fill it, most appropriately, with forget-me-nots and fresh baby's breath. Then I put it and the doll-sized teaset on the miniature desk that has the date 1837 written on the back in a bold hand. They are quite at home in the same spot where, I am sure, they sat once upon a time, long, long ago.

Outside of your grandmother's attic, you can find beautiful containers and treasures in antique shops and flea markets wherever you may travel. When I find one I can't resist *and* the price is only a fraction of its real value, you can be sure I'm going to snatch it up, no matter where it is!

Containers do not have to be designed for holding flowers. The violets on this hand-painted demitasse cup and saucer (above) are so realistic you can hardly distinguish them from the real thing. Who would guess that this bunny and lettuce bowl (right) was intended to be a soup bowl. And I've never used this English creamware sauce boat (opposite) for anything but flowers.

That's what I did when I found a simple English nineteenth-century creamware sauce boat marked $20 in a small Carmel, California, antiques shop. To a serious collector its price could be ten times that amount. To me it is "priceless" because it is perfect to hold bluish-purple bachelor's buttons, yellow Boston daisies, and that staple of my garden, the green Lenten Rose that blooms from December to May. Now, when friends or family come to stay, I arrange the flowers just the way I want them in my sauce boat and put them on the bedside table in the guest bedroom.

Several years ago, while walking along another inviting shopping scene,

New York's Fifty-seventh Street, I commanded myself over and over, "Window-shop only. Do not go into any stores. You do not need another thing!"

I was heeding my own admonitions quite well when the cutest little pottery bunny I had ever seen caught my eye. Despite my resolve, I suddenly found myself *inside* the shop, clearly saying, "They're soup bowls? How charming. Do you have four?" followed in a heartbeat by those irretractable words, "How soon can you ship them?"

Every spring those still-adorable soup bowls come out of the china closet to be used for everything from spinach dip to Easter candy to, of course,

"Winter's done, and April's in the skies, Earth, look up with laughter in your eyes."

~

Charles G. D. Roberts

This whimsical clothes sprinkler was a permanent fixture on the basement windowsill of my parents' home during those days of starched little-girl pinafores and yard-wide damask napkins. Though practically no one under forty even knows what a clothes sprinkler is, it's a shame to hide this cheerful fellow away.

flowers—cheerful narcissi, bright-eyed pansies, creamy buttercups, the very first day lily plucked from the garden, a touch of velvety silver lamb's ear, and a special treat for bunny to nibble on, a healthy bunch of homegrown parsley. They never have been used for soup.

I have many other garden-container treasures tucked away waiting for the perfect occasion for me to use them. Not long ago I came into the house feeling somewhat despondent after a few stolen minutes in the garden when I should have been tending to the day-old paperwork piled on my desk. Oh, I wasn't sad at having to leave my garden. It had done its magic. I was refreshed

and restored, my mind filled with new ideas and images. Rather, I was feeling bad because I knew tomorrow the grass had to be mowed and there was no way to save the cheerful Johnny-jump-ups that had, true to their names, jumped up and over the stone edging of the garden and appeared overnight in the tall grassy lawn. They joined their cousin violets that had overnight turned my green lawn into a purple cloth.

If only they both had stayed within the rock edging that borders my flower bed they would have grown taller, with stronger stalks. Then I could have put them in thimble-size silver cordial glasses I seldom use except for miniature flowers. But as they were, their short stems had been choked out by the stronger clumps of grass.

Suddenly, I remembered my collection of demitasse cups packed away in the bottom drawer of the chest in the guest bedroom. Wasn't there a cup and saucer painted with violets or pansies or some such? At the back of the corner cupboard I found the lovely hand-painted demitasse cup and saucer my Texas friend Ruth Little had painted for me several years ago.

The violets' lilac-colored and rose-tinted faces blended perfectly with those on the cup. Like so many pleasures that we come upon unexpectedly, together the tiny blossoms and miniature cup added great cheer to my day—as did the four-leaf clover that I never would have found if I hadn't stopped to rescue my adventuresome little flowers.

*M*any a generation of little girls have found these miniature pieces (above) just right for the tiny flowers their mothers could never use in a large vase.

*B*eautifully hand-painted vases decorated with everlasting flowers (right) are cheerful reminders of spring's garden year round.

When my petunias got leggy and straggly I snipped the top blossoms off and put them in a seashell brought back from the beach. What could be easier?

"Who bends a knee where violets grow A hundred secret things shall know." ～ Rachel Field

A WORKING WOMAN'S FLOWERS

～

My garden is a small, working woman's garden filled with simple flowers and familiar faces. There are pansies and phlox in the spring, asters and marigolds in the summer, chrysanthemums in the fall, and snowdrops and crocuses in the winter. And impatiens—red, white, pink, coral, fuchsia, raspberry, and even orange.

I have a garden for simple reasons. I love to dig in the earth and create a little place of beauty that I can call my own. Flowers and greenery of every season brighten my days regardless of what

else is going on in the world and my garden cheers me on when nothing else can. To me a day without a posy of some sort nearby on my desk or work table truly is a day without sunshine. You may have my wine, but leave me my flower.

When I'm away from home, as is so often the case, I still try to have at least one flower in my hotel room. Long ago I learned that, like my flowers at home, I, too, must be nurtured. So sometimes I buy a rose or bunch of flowers from the hotel gift shop or the deli around the corner. Other times, to the horror and embarrassment of my dinner companions, I have been known to snip a blossom from the centerpiece. I've even pinched off a fading blossom from a hotel-lobby arrangement. But I also recycle flowers when I can. In hotel hallways I keep an eagle eye out for room service trays piled high with dirty dishes and a wilting pink carnation. When no one is looking I slip by, snatch the poor carnation up, and give it a new and much more appreciative home by my bed.

Those times when I'm in one location for three or so days I make an earnest attempt to buy a potted plant of some sort. A long-lasting chrysanthemum or frilly petaled African violet usually costs no more than five or six dollars, and makes a delightful gift for the maid or bellboy to take home. On my trips from city to city, when I am presented with a corsage, a bouquet, or a basket of flowers, I drag them home, ribbons and all, and keep them until, while I'm away again, someone weeds out my collection. Liza thinks I don't notice, but I do.

And I never return home without a half-dead and crushed flower at the bottom of my purse or a few blossoms pressed in whatever book I'm reading. These go up on the bulletin board above my desk, get tucked into the window blinds in front of my computer table, or are scattered all around to remind me of people and places, sights and sounds, conversations and experiences—tangible, yet fragile, memories of life's riches.

I rob my own garden of just enough flowers to stick in a little bud vase or simple bowl. I grow flowers and herbs for their colors, fragrances, shapes, and textures. As a working woman I prefer to spend any spare time among my flowers, either working in the garden or fixing flowers to share with my family and guests. Unlike my mother, who delighted in creating perfect, award-winning flower arrangements, my own favorite arrangement is best described as "flowers in a bowl." My simple flower garden

provides all the right ingredients. And when I need exquisite royal-blue delphinium, elegant long-stemmed red roses, and perfectly formed virginal-white calla lilies I call Carlton Long. That's what florists are for.

Because my work often takes me from my garden for weeks at a time, I must have a low-maintenance flower garden—another reason for growing time-tested flowers. Over the years I have found that once the ground is prepared—tilled, enriched with peat moss, manure,

*H*anging baskets are wonderful! After adding color on the patio for a spring party, these profusely blooming petunias will add cheer to the garden throughout the summer.

I love flowers that can be moved around the garden for special effect. Vegetable baskets and cast-iron pots lend a rustic touch.

fertilizers, or loam soil—planting a garden in the spring really takes only two days. The heavy preparation is a one-time job. I am speaking only about caring for the flower border, not about a front or backyard that has to be seeded, watered, and mowed and mowed and mowed. It takes most of a day to clear and clean the winter debris away, half a day to buy the plants and seeds, and another half day to arrange and plant them. What rewards those two days yield for months to come!

When I am out of town and the garden gets shabby from too much sun and heat, too little water, and not enough of me, hanging baskets can provide instant garden magic upon my return. Baskets are a wonderful shortcut to having a spectacular display of colors and fresh blossoms when and where you need them. Bend down the wire hangers and sink beautiful hanging baskets into the ground to create the appearance of abundant garden-grown plants on demand. Later, these baskets can be hung in a suitable place or moved from spot to spot for great variety. Just remember, hanging baskets dry out quickly and need more watering than your permanently planted garden. But their versatility and endless profusion of blooms are well worth the extra care.

"Go forth, my little daughter,
The mid-day heat is o'er
Go forth among the flowers,
And gather thee a store."

Anonymous

A more formal air is achieved by placing a row of hanging baskets and an arrangement of spring flowers among hosta and lirope beds.

"What men or gods are these? What maidens loth?

What mad pursuit? What struggle to escape?

What pipes and timbrels? What wild ecstasy?"

"Ode on a Grecian Urn," John Keats

GARDEN ORNAMENTS

*J*n long silent rows they stood bathed in sunlight, cooled by shadows. Gods and goddesses, satyrs and nymphs, poets and lovers, shepherds and shepherdesses of another time and another place, frozen in time, were captured in stone—allegorical and mythological symbols of life's many moods, its pleasures, its despairs, its everyday tasks, its grand

shop I made my decision out of frustration. I began by taking some panoramic shots. But peering through the camera lens I soon noticed little details my eye had not seen—exquisitely formed fingers, a disarranged curl, an evocative smile. I moved closer, seeing more and more.

Only the pedestaled statues remained stationary. A gentle wind wove among the tree branches swaying a leaf here and there. The light and shadows constantly changed as the clouds and the wind played hide-and seek with one another. I raced to find the perfect light, the perfect scene, the perfect angle—when quietly and most mysteriously these fanciful stone monuments created long ago in imitation of ourselves began to come to

At the Huntington Gardens in Pasadena, California, beautifully sculpted figures allegorically speak of life's pleasures and endeavors.

celebrations. Visually the garden was breathtaking; intellectually it was challenging; emotionally it was soul-stirring.

I longed to wander, to let my thoughts be free, to dream, to take in the majesty and awe I felt in the presence of so much beauty, but time was short. The gates of the Huntington Botanical Gardens soon would open to the public. Tourists and visitors would be everywhere. The staff, knowing my time to photograph in the gardens was limited, had been more than helpful. They told me where to go, what shortcuts to take, where the most abundant blooms were. But, they said, there were restrictions. When the gardens officially opened I must not obstruct the visitors' enjoyment. Do not ask anyone to move or not get in your way, they said pointedly.

The minutes were ticking away. Where should I begin? Everywhere I looked were wonderful images I longed to capture. Like the kid in the candy

life. As I moved to catch a smiling lip here, a downcast glance there, I was swept up in feelings of shared intimacy with these figures.

I knew that courtier's wry glance. I understood the peasant girl's demure look. I felt the joy of the romping, carefree child perched atop the water fountain. I thrilled to the lovers' embrace.

A rich, transcendent sensation rose from deep in my heart. Every nerve ending in my body tingled. It was as if I were living all my life in that one moment. I felt as one with the world and at peace with myself.

Suddenly, muffled voices in the distance interrupted my exquisite feelings and the silence of the place. Chatter and laughter were all around me. I listened. It

was a foreign tongue. I couldn't understand the words, but I could interpret their meanings.

Putting down my camera, I watched a wave of Oriental tourists stream across the green lawn toward me. Their eyes twinkled. Their hands danced through the air gesturing toward the statues. As one body, the group stopped before the first majestic figure. One woman whispered to another, her words spoken behind a cupped hand while she pointed toward the stone sculpture with the other hand. Others chatted loudly. Everyone's conversation was spirited and lively.

The scene was a study in cultural contrasts. Small, delicate, animated Eastern people stood before bigger-than-life motionless European statues. Every physical detail of their Oriental and Occidental features was different —the hair, the eyes, the mouths, even their bodies and carriage. In that moment I sensed a

Light and shadows that cast ever-changing patterns on stone and foliage alike enhance our joy in the visual pleasures of fleeting moments in the garden.

universal language flowing between the observers and those stone visages—a language of feelings rather than words—a language of human emotions and life experiences that transcends physical differences that exist among the races or peoples of the world.

Long ago poets and philosophers in every country of the world created inspiring legends to tell us about ourselves—stories of commonly shared emotions and experiences, tales of love and life, greed and generosity, tragedy and joy—myths to help us understand what we feel and how we think. Since time immemorial artists have fashioned stone and marble, bronze and lead into human images to capture in a face, a pose, or gesture, the pathos all mankind feels, but which few can express.

Is Cupid placing or removing the scarf? Is love blind or in love do we see truth? Life's universal mysteries transcend time and place.

I know of no more fitting place to retell these stories than in the garden, where we are surrounded by life's mysteries. I know of no other images that evoke such immediate understanding of life's complexities as classical garden sculpture. Even the most humble spirit soars in the presence of beautiful, symbolic images.

Content with my thoughts, but aware of the time, I moved from my partially hidden perch just as the group began proceeding to the next figure. For the first time they saw me. They smiled and bowed politely, the way the Oriental people do. I smiled and waved back, the way we Americans do.

As the day progressed the gardens became filled with people of every description and with every purpose—tourists and sightseers, foreigners and natives, serious gardeners and garden hobbyists, artists with sketchbooks underarm, children with babysitters, sun worshipers, multigenerational families, and of course other photographers, professional and amateur. Despite the crowds and the diversity of the people, I never once even thought of asking anyone to move or wait. And no one ever disturbed me by walking between my camera and my subject. Surrounded by beauty, everyone was patient—giving and taking without so much as a fitful or cross word. Instinctively we each seemed to know that in the presence of more pageantry than our senses could inhale there was no need to be greedy.

Late in the afternoon, as I wound my way toward the exit, once again I passed the long row of figures where I had started out that morning. I felt a sharp pang of regret that the day and my adventure had to end. What if I were to slip among the bushes and hide, I thought in a moment of passion. Would the figures step down from their pedestals in the moonlight of this midsummer June night? Would Pan's pipes be heard through the trees? Would Daphne romp among the nymphs? Would

Narcissus slip through the woods to the mirror-clear pond to admire himself? Would the shepherdesses gather a mantle of flowers to drape around the shepherds? I would never know.

But tomorrow promised to be another glorious day. I was going to another garden specifically created as a place for leisure and to celebrate the creative spirit of man through garden sculpture.

How different my experience there turned out to be. It was not at all what I expected.

Oh, the grounds were lovely, well manicured and green. The gently rolling expanse of lawn was filled with sculptures, but they were modern bronze and steel, aluminum, plaster, and ceramic pieces. Rough-textured, free-form sculptures and masses of molten metal were within only a few feet of you, no matter where you stood or sat. Irregular and jarring geometric forms piled one on the other were mounted on white concrete bases sunk into the green grass. Nude female forms in various stages of repose and impatience stood guard.

Unlike yesterday there were no crowds, not even anyone to disturb, at least until the noon hour arrived. Then a few office workers sauntered out from nearby brick and glass buildings carrying lunch bags. A few stopped and sat on the benches along the walkways. One couple ventured on to the grass where, cross-legged, they ate in silence. I chuckled as I watched one bearded gentleman, no doubt a learned professor, book in hand, stretch out beneath a dark-barked fir tree, open his book, and promptly doze off.

I was astonished by the silence and passiveness of the scene I was witnessing. It was a beautiful Los Angeles day— the sort that made you want to whistle or hum. The azure sky was cloudless. It was a day to inspire poets and entice even the most diligent bureaucrat to go home, putter around the garden, hit a few golf balls, or go to the beach. I listened for happy voices. I searched the faces of those I saw for smiles and laughing eyes. I

From majestic fountains to images of childhood innocence, classical garden sculpture is poetic and poignant.

BANNERS
AND FESTIVE
FLAGS

$\mathcal{M}$illie Jones, of Richmond, Virginia, was looking for a special way to announce the birth of her baby boy. She came upon the bright idea of hanging out a banner and turned it into a thriving business. These days she and people everywhere are dressing their doorways, patios, gazebos, and decks with welcoming, celebratory, festive flags. Here are just a few of the banners I have particularly admired on my travels through the year. They have a charm as special and individual as that of any garden ornament.

heard none. I saw none. The scene was not one of joy or even peace. It was somber, tomblike.

Suddenly a little fellow, no more than two-and-a-half, came bounding down a path, his youthful mother close behind. He squealed with delight as he ran toward a huge sculpture in the middle of the court, the sort of piece that begs to be climbed on. His youthful, joyful noises were the first break in the quiet of the garden I had heard the entire time I had spent walking and searching for some form of beauty, some sense of exuberant expression.

His romp turned into a gallop. His chubby little hands clutched a protruding rod as he began his upward climb. But his squeals of delight were instantly drowned out by his mother's angry shouts

at him. Get down! When he didn't respond she jerked him down and dragged him back to the walk.

So this is beauty, I thought to myself on that perfect day in the midst of a place created for leisure and enhanced by modern garden sculpture. Maybe I am the one at fault, I told myself. Look harder. Have an open mind. I tried as hard as I could. Finally, after passing one lifeless sculpture after another, I paused before a sculpture that to me resembled an open pouch with two oranges about to spill out. The only image I could envision was that of a Christmas stocking, though the ginko-leaf-like ornament in front of a circle suggested I should be thinking in broader terms. "Look at the plaque and stop guessing," I chastised myself. "Artemis of Ephesus," I read.

In the 17th century King Henry IV of France wrote, "What is the existence of man's life? It is a dial which points out The sunset as it moves about: And shadows out, in lines of night, The subtle changes of time's flight; Till all obscuring Earth hath laid The body in perpetual shade."

Garden ornaments can also be playful and whimsical. On my travels many a gray day has been brightened when an imaginative decoration has caught my eye. From a bushy green billy goat gruff (left) to Bob Timberlake's artistic arrangements of three gernaniums on an abandoned wagon part (right), mirth is one of garden's many joys.

PAN'S GARDEN

Oh, Happy little piping Pan—
There, in your garden close,
Shadowed by spruce boughs interlaced,
Fragrant with breath of rose—

Although your pipes are silent long,
I love to think you wait
Till evening folds your garden in,
Behind the rustic gate;

And then you play your pipes again;
And, by the fireflies' light,
Elves leap from every flower's heart,
And throng the musky night!

All day you watch the flagstones, set
Within your aisle of green—
With pipes uplifted, listening
Till twilight comes, serene!

Bertha Bolling

Artemis . . . Artemis . . . Suddenly a tidbit of information I had learned from a book that had been required college reading emerged from the deep recesses of my brain. "Artemis, also known as the Diana, the beautiful fleet huntress, exquisite in the light of the moon," I half spoke to myself.

Diana . . . Diana . . . I walked around the abstract bronze temple that still looked like an open pouch with two oranges about to spill out. I could find no line of beauty. Despite its allusiveness, there was no mystery. It held no intrigue. It was like an obscure intellectual riddle—you either got the point of the sculpture or you didn't. I looked through the camera lens thinking maybe I had missed something. I hadn't. It was then I noticed I had not taken a picture the entire morning. Yesterday, after just one hour, I had shot five 36-exposure rolls of film.

How ironic, I thought. Yesterday, I, and hundreds of visitors, had thrilled to the beauty and mystery of sculpture created by artists whose names we would never know, but whose works inspired us to laughter and smiles. As I walked through that garden I had felt the human heart beat. But today, among these confusing abstract forms of steel and aluminum, I felt nothing but indifference. I realized then that we don't need reminders of chaos and tangled lives in the garden. Our lives are already filled with enough problems and stresses. The garden should be a place of joy and beauty, a place of wonder, a place of poetry and images that stir our hearts and inspire us.

My thoughts were so clear. Yet, as often happens, later that day when I tried to express them, my words fell short. Then I remembered a few simple lines of poetry. Like those unknown and long-forgotten artists who sculpted the allegorical and mythological gods and goddesses, satyrs and nymphs, poets and lovers, shepherds and shepherdesses of another time and another place, the poet who wrote these lines is also unknown, but his words remain poignant:

I gaze upon the garden.
My heart grown peaceful.
From its spirit comes my will.
From its color comes my being.

Sheltered by a canopy of red camellias, youth's shyness and melancholy are captured to last through all of life's seasons.

𝒲ho has not taken a heart full of worries into the garden only to leave there renewed and restored? Every garden should have a place to meditate, a place where gloom can be left behind and life set aright.

163

CEMETERY GARDENS

"As for man, his days are as grass:
as a flower of the field, so he flourisheth.
For the wind passeth over it, and it is gone;
and the place thereof shall know it no more."

Psalm 103:15–16

Few people other than garden historians know that many of America's first public gardens and parks were her cemeteries. Now, before you jump over this section thinking this is going to be morbid, consider this. Many of America's most beautiful cemeteries actually grew out of our ancestors' wish to create a place of beauty to heal the body as well as feed the spirit.

"Cemetery parks" as they were called, became prominent in the early nineteenth century when civic leaders of overcrowded cities began asking, Where are the children going to play? Where can hardworking men and women, after spending long daylight hours in dark, closed-up factories and shops, renew their spirits and soak up the fresh air and sunshine so essential to their physical health?

A guardian angel adds grace to the gardens of Monmouth in Natchez, Mississippi.

At the same time, a problem facing the cities was where to bury the dead. Family burial plots and small country church graveyards back home were of no good to the people who had moved from their farms and villages to far-away cities.

Out of these seemingly very different concerns—a park for leisure time and a graveyard—came the concept of a beautiful green space that could both enrich the lives of the living and serve as a resting place for the departed.

In the early 1830s the Massachusetts Horticultural Society heartily endorsed creating "a rural cemetery and experimental garden" in Boston. Named Mount Auburn after the idealistic village "Sweet Auburn! loveliest village of the plain," in Oliver Goldsmith's 1770 poem "The Deserted Village," this "cemetery park" was immediately successful. Soon beautifully landscaped cemetery parks enclosed by impressive iron fences and gates sprang up everywhere. The finest ones were designed with meandering paths, winding streams, quiet ponds, stone benches, and charming gazebos. Even the more modest graveyards were filled with lovely flowers, cheerful birds, and, of course, towering evergreens and oak trees. Whether large or small, cemeteries were perceived as bucolic, even very romantic places.

But as they grew in popularity, their peacefulness became threatened. Riders on horseback and visitors in carriages impeded lovers' intimate strolls. Young children could no longer safely frolic around on the greens. Furthermore, the horses kicked up dust and wore down the roads. Recklessly driven carriages trampled the grass along the pathways and destroyed the carefully planted borders. Over weekends and holidays such large throngs assembled among the graves that some cemeteries eventually passed rules banning picnics and parties altogether.

After all, cemeteries were also meant to be sacred sanctuaries—places where, in quietness and serenity, all manner of people could contemplate their own mortality, a concept of grave concern to the Victorians. In these cemeteries where their families were buried, the rich and the poor alike could commune with nature, speak to God, and, most significantly, ponder life's meanings all the while fully aware that eventually this would be their final home, too.

Whether for good or for bad, we have lost these dual traditions of the cemetery park. These days so many "modern" cemeteries conveniently built close to highways for easy access are insipid, undistinguished acres of treeless earth. There are no monuments that tell rich histories and recall a dear departed's favorite line or two of poetry. No trees give shelter to birds. The only visible flowers are plastic. The earth is devoid of any signs of life other than the monotonous carpet of perfectly manicured grass. Who would even want to stroll through this environment?

But in all fairness, given the choice, why should we today spend our leisure time in a dreary old cemetery, even ones with beautiful sculpture and primeval

trees, when we can jump in our cars and whiz along the interstate highways to get to the beach or the mountains?

At no time and in no place are we more aware of life's bountiful gifts than when we are surrounded by century-old trees, their limbs providing sheltering canopies for weather-worn monuments and headstones and, at the same time, a home to fledging birds who have just

Our nineteenth-century ancestors' cemeteries were planned to be beautiful parks, masterfully landscaped with winding paths, beautiful monuments, and primeval trees.

During the early years of the twentieth century, with the coming of automobiles and a more mobile society, the popularity of cemetery parks waned. But great philanthropists reared in that earlier tradition established many beautiful sanctuaries. Here at the Henry Francis du Pont Winterthur Gardens in Delaware, we can still find solace and commune with nature and contemplate our inner thoughts and feelings.

left their parents' nest, and are about to begin a new life of their own.

Life is filled with wonderful mysteries, but when we lose awareness of life's eventual end we take these all for granted. The ancients said, Let the dead bury the dead. We today say, Life is for the living. Both messages urge us to live life to its fullest.

Through the ages the poets and wise men have told us, much more lyrically than I can, that our lives are made rich, even noble, by sharing and loving. The fulfilled life comes to those people who delight in little joys, to those who join in others' laughter, to those who see beyond themselves, their problems, and their own shortcomings.

When looking at the various and wondrous plants and flowers planted in the gardens of the world, each one different, each one special in its own way, I see much we should remember in our own lives. Even a simple garden becomes a metaphor for life's larger picture.

In our gardens we can always manage to find a place for both the shy, tender, blue-eyed forget-me-not and the ever-sturdy but oftentimes shaggy, bright-blossomed zinnia. Can't we find room in our lives to embrace those people who are different from us?

And what about ourselves? Where do we fit into another's garden? Some of us seek a quiet life. We wish to be as retiring and endearing as the tender impatiens plant, which is at its best in reflected light and shade. Others of us harbor ambitions to be as showy and flamboyant as the vibrant dahlia, which must have full sun to grow and thrives amid adversity. We would do well to remember that the zinnia cannot be the impatien or vice versa, and each plant will grow best only in the appropriate setting.

Looking around my garden, I think about what a different place it is at different times, according to my own needs. I retreat to the garden to be alone, to find solitude. Yet there is nothing I enjoy more than filling my quiet garden with boisterous laughter and noise when friends come over for a cookout or a party. My garden has room for serenity and for frivolity.

In our lives we begin each day by waking from a quiet sleep to face life's frantic reality. As we go through routine daily tasks in our workaday world we seek to return to our sleeping hours as we dream of romance and rapture. So many people today seem to add great unhappiness to their lives because they want life to be ideal. They only want to live a dream. How much more content they would be if they would remember that we must make room for both the real and the dream, the dark and the bright, in our lives.

To be like the daffodils and tulips, which burst into glory in the springtime and have sparkling bright moments, we too must endure a winter of silence and aloneness. To have the fullest blossom for our hour in the sun, first we must spread our roots in the cold dark earth.

Looking around my garden I realize that, quite simply, life is its own reward. There is absolutely nothing wrong with enjoying beauty for beauty's sake.

That's why, long ago, our ancestors created the cemetery park where everyone could find peace in quiet moments and delight in having fun, where lovers could plan for the future and mourners could remember the past, and where the old and the young, the rich and the poor could spend precious hours of their lives surrounded by the beauty and splendor of the garden.

～

"Ah yet, ere I descend to the grave
May I a small house and large garden have…"
"The Wish," Abraham Cowley

In a small New England cemetery, flags, flowers, and tombstones are silent vestiges of lives past and present.

"Two roads diverged in a wood, and I—
I took the one less traveled by,
And that has made all the difference."
"The Road Less Traveled," Robert Frost

THE WELL-TRAVELED ROAD

But not every road must be less traveled to be magical. Almost everyone has a road well traveled, year after year, that has a specialness all its own. For you it may be the secret shortcut you take home from work each day that winds through a quiet neighborhood where the houses line up just right. For another it is the short block just around the corner where the branches of a single, majestic oak form a year-round canopy over the sidewalk. For me it is a stretch of highway that links the past with today—a road from my house to my parents' home.

I know every inch of Route 86 from Danville, Virginia, to Raleigh, North Carolina, by heart. Or from Raleigh to Danville. It all depends on whether you're traveling north to south or south to north. In either direction, I can tell you before each bend where the wild azaleas will be blooming in early April. And where the goldenrod and black-eyed Susans will be out in late August. They give the green fields and my spirits a golden glow. I know where the cows will be wading in the shallow pond in mid-July's stifling heat and where to expect new kittens to be frolicking in May.

I've often wondered whether we build birdhouses for the birds or ourselves.

I have traveled this road every hour of the night and day for the past forty-plus years. And this road knows me as well as I know it, for as I have traveled those gently rolling Piedmont hills and knolls I have dreamed dreams, wept secret tears, thrilled with joyful expectation, and struggled to keep awake. My moods have been as varied as have

my reasons for traveling along the road.

During the 1940s and early 1950s my adored maternal grandparents lived in Raleigh. My parents and I lived in Danville. At least one Sunday a month we drove to Raleigh for a visit. Those bright, sunny trips (at least, that's how I remember them) were filled with a quiet, secure excitement and a child's expectations. The miles whizzed by.

Somehow, Mamma and Papa always heard our Studebaker turn into their backyard driveway. Before we could get out of the car they rushed out to meet us. After hugs and kisses I knew that inside, fun-filled times and the best biscuits in the world were waiting.

Sunset, a melancholy time anyway, signaled it was time to leave. How the miles dragged as we drove back to Danville. Though Mother and Daddy sang songs and told funny stories to keep my spirits up, I traveled those late twilight and nighttime trips in the lonesome sadness every child learns early in life when separated from the people he or she loves.

During the late 1950s many changes came to be. First, Papa died. Then Mamma moved away. In those days we went to Raleigh only for business, shopping, and cemetery visits. Then, by chance or fate, in 1962 I married "a Raleigh boy," as we in the South say.

As he and I drove Route 86 together I delighted in telling my new husband about my many childhood trips along that road and all about my grandfather, whom he would never know except through stories. Happily chatting away, I

$\mathscr{A}$long the roadside, nature's wild flowers are lovely to glimpse as you pass by.

still took the moment to notice how the sun laid long shadows across the ever-green-lined edge of the unplanted winter fields, or how the red clay clumped together along the side of the road after a heavy summer thunderstorm.

Eventually we left the South and moved to Wisconsin, but home beckons to everyone. In 1970 Clauston took a job in Raleigh. Twenty-plus years after those never-to-be-forgotten childhood trips I began repeating the familiar once-a-month drive along Route 86. This time, however, the trip was from Raleigh to Danville. And this time I was driving *my children* to see *their* grandparents. Soon Langdon and Joslin learned the same twisting curves and straight stretches I had known those many years ago.

What grand adventures we had! One day, as we approached the swampy part of the road where Lynch Creek slithers around the bend, I had to slam on the brakes to let a huge buzzard, his blood-red tenons clutching the longest black snake I've ever seen, lift off from the ever-perilous highway and soar into the sky, taking his prize home to his family safe in the deep woods. In awe, we marveled at this usually disgusting bird of prey's beauty as his outstretched wings, jet black in the shimmering sunlight, lifted him gracefully into his flight.

Another time, one December night, just as the red sun set in the west and the silver winter moon rose in the east, we slowed down to admire a grand twelve-point deer poised momentarily at the edge of the forest.

In many a deserted country yard a cluster of iris, or daffodils perhaps, remain to bloom unnoticed.

Our city family delighted in those country experiences. But there were the many other times one of us would sadly remark, "Oh dear, they're clearing out those woods over there. Bet we'll see a new house before long." Sure enough, the next time we'd drive past, piles of lumber and bricks and sometimes even a nearby city realtor's sign were where the maples and pines had been.

At least along a country road those inevitable changes come slowly enough that they can be watched. To me that's important. New houses still go up one at a time. Carpenters and bricklayers in overalls still work from sunrise till sundown. Once finished, though, you can always tell the newly built houses from the old ones. The new ones are built close to the road and close to one another. The old houses are set back from the road with long, tree-lined driveways and have thick woods in the far-distant backyard. In the summer months you see only the driveways, not the houses.

Another familiar sight along the country road are those deserted homeplaces that are left standing empty when a family moves on. It takes years for a vacated house or barn to deteriorate. Eventually they fall down under the choking weight of the trumpet vine, ivy, and kudzu that weave through the windows and around the chimney. But they are never taken down, much less blown up.

In the city, noble buildings are imploded in ten seconds and prefab skyscrapers seem to spring up in their places overnight. The single push of a remote-control button set off on late Friday afternoon to avoid rush-hour traffic can demolish a nineteenth-century edifice painstakingly built by craftsmen who laid bricks one by one. The rubble is immediately hauled away. By sunrise Monday morning, cranes are in place, poised to heave ready-to-assemble beams into place. In the country, even long after the timbers have collapsed and the bricks begun to crumble, the gardens remain.

Each spring patches of pink and lavender phlox still spread along the bank that once separated the gully by the road from the front yard. Crepe myrtle trees still burst into bloom by the Fourth of July in what once was a side yard. A long-neglected, ungroomed, and unkempt rambling rose bush continues to put out fragrant bouquets of sweetheart blossoms all summer long. And the ageratum grows taller and wilder each fall. How much pleasure these spots of beauty continue to give to all who pass by and take the time to notice them.

One sweltering hot early August day when twilight would last far into the night, instead of pushing the speed limit—and my luck—I slowed down. I took in the simple beauty of the countryside. Soon the lifelong kinship I had felt with those many houses and yards along that stretch of road got the best of me. I wondered what would happen if I drove up the driveways I knew so well, knocked on the doors, and met the people who lived there.

In my relaxed, contemplative state I glimpsed a whimsical, homemade sign.

It might have been there all along, but I had never noticed it before—probably because I was going too fast or my eyes were too busy taking in all the flowers around it. The name on the homemade Dutch girl and boy plaque jumped out at me. THE.WILEY,S.

You see, over the years the Wileys' grand array of riotous magenta cockscombs, irresistible ruffly hollyhocks, cheerful zinnias, and Jack-and-the-beanstalk-tall cannas had given me great delight. But I had never known the name of the people who grew them. Now I did. What would happen, I wondered, if I stopped, rang the doorbell, and said to the Wileys, "Hello, I'm Emyl Jenkins. I've always loved your garden." That's just what I did.

Nace and Addie Wiley retired some time back from the workaday world, but visiting with friends, minding chores, keeping up with their family, and tending their garden fill their days. I think they truly welcomed this stranger who interrupted their early lunch. Together we wandered around their side yard,

In the Wileys' yard, glorious coxcombs are nature's cultivated colors at their most brilliant.

strangers now friends, sharing stories, memories, and flowers.

In the sanctuary of a garden, it seems natural to share our inner thoughts. That's why, while admiring Addie's hollyhocks, I admitted that the house of my dreams is a simple, picturesque cottage surrounded by a never-chipped, always spanking-white, picket fence bordered by rows of old-fashioned seven-foot-tall hollyhocks. In my dreams the tips of every princely spire bend low, full and heavy with wide-opened deep-throated salmon and yellow blossoms where the butterflies dance all day.

My cottage is a dream. So are the hollyhocks. Never once have I persuaded the short, very expensive hollyhock plants I have brought home from the nursery year after year to grow one bit—much less bud or blossom—no matter how properly or carefully I plant them. Maybe it's my fence's fault. It's wrought-iron and painted black—not wooden and white. Or maybe it is because I *bought* the plants. Dwarfed by her full-blossomed, skyscraping hollyhocks, Addie Wiley confessed to me that she hadn't bought hers.

Eventually this old shack will crumble under the weight of the trumpet vine that twists through its timbers, but for now its weathered red roof is lovely wrapped in green.

"You know," she confided in soft tones, "I *stole* the first one. I was in a garden and there was a sign that said, 'Do Not Touch.' That was a written invitation to snitch a piece! I had a tissue tucked in my bra. So I reached right over, snipped off a seedpod, hid it away in the tissue, and brought it home and sprinkled the seeds. If you'll come back in the fall I'll give you some hollyhock slips. I'd love to share my plants with you."

I left the Wileys' garden, already looking forward to a return visit in the fall. Buoyant in my new-found braveness I knew exactly where I was going next.

Route 86 is a plain road. Even the occasional two-story nineteenth-century farmhouses with acreage around them can in no way be described as antebellum mansions or "Tara-esque." Among the many modest red-brick houses that dot the landscape, one always catches my eye. It's the one with the old-timey well perched front and center on the grassy rise that separates the house from the highway. Even from the road you can tell it isn't a real water-drawing well. It has stone edging and there are sturdy marigolds and petunias planted around it. But it is cheerful in its simplicity and it told me something about the people who live there even before I met them. I knew they would be neighborly.

I wasn't disappointed. When Brenda Johnson opened the door and saw my sweaty brow (even a ten-minute drive with the car's air conditioning blowing full blast won't cool you down after an hour in a garden in the blistering summer

Southern heat), she invited me in before I could tell her who I was and why I was knocking at her door. "It's much too hot to stand out there and talk," she said, her voice as hospitable as her smile. But I convinced her it was the outside I wanted to know about. So she, her teen-aged daughter, Jennifer, and toddler nephew, Raymond, joined me for a closer look at the decorative well her father, Darrnell Stephens, had built, "just because he likes to make things." Then she showed me the settee and chairs he had made to match the well.

These days, I keep an eager eye out to see if anything new has been added to the yard for I now know the family who lives in this house. I wave to growing Raymond when I see him out in the yard, though he has no idea who I am. I didn't meet Brenda's father that day, but each time I drive by I think about him and the hours it took to make the garden ornaments that set this rural house apart from the others around it.

I had cooled off, at least a little, by the time I got to the next stop on my own magical mystery tour. Nevertheless the Hancocks, another retired couple, offered me a cooling lemonade. While we sat on the porch steps of the 1851 farmhouse sheltered by a primeval half-mile-wide tree, the Hancocks told me what I had stopped to learn about—the cloud-touching birdhouses I always admired from the road.

Once they stood tall and straight. That was before they endured many seasons of high winds and sweeping

rains. Now, like the deserted barns and houses along the road, they lean and tilt, totter and sway. And the birds don't seem to come as often these days either. Odell Hancock told me the snakes have run off the martins.

But the hummingbirds still come, Elsie, his wife, said, as a single bird zoomed from the limb of a distant bush, seemingly froze in midair, and then

Along country roads deliciously fragrant vines of wild honeysuckle and ancient boughs hung heavy with ripened pears make us long for an earlier and simpler time.

much larger," Elsie added. Indeed, the pint-sized hummingbird crochets its nest from tiny snips of moldy green tree bark, gossamer spider-web threads, and its own saliva. That year, when the baby hummingbirds hatched and the nest was left empty, the Hancocks took this seldom-seen birdhouse to a local museum for the schoolchildren to learn from and marvel at. My own education was widely expanded that day.

As I left, the Hancocks earnestly thanked me for "coming by" and asked me to stay longer, but there was one last stop to be made before the threatening summer rain moved in from the west— the little rock village.

Imagine, if you can, a miniature town of houses, stores, an inn, a mill, even a "burlesque" show and "necessary house," all made of stone and just the right size for every little boy and girl under seven years old. With a Coke in his hand and a cigarette in his mouth, Henry Warren began building this Caswell County, North Carolina, Lilliputian wonderland in 1968, the year Langdon was born in far-away Wisconsin. The summer Langdon was two and we were once again living in Raleigh, we practiced farm words and sounds like *moo* and *horse* and *gitty-up* as we drove along Route 86 to and from his grandparents' home.

Back then the village was so close to the highway you had only to pull off onto the soft shoulder and you stepped out of the car into a fantasy world. We often stopped, for if every little girl should know the wonder of a life-sized

*A*udubon said the shimmering metallic green hummingbird resembles "a glittering fragment of a rainbow."

imperceptibly sipped drops of sugar water from the recently filled feeder near us. In one voice, Odell and Elsie recalled how they had patiently waited and watched the hummingbirds zigzag from tree to bush to branch to limb all one summer until they figured out where their nest was. "You'd never find one if you didn't follow the hummingbirds," Odell said. "Why, when the eggs hatch, the baby birds are no larger than the first joint of your thumb. Their nest isn't

doll house, every little boy should know the fun of a built-to-scale village. I've never seen a boy yet who didn't love to build. After a romp up and down the steps of each little building, when we got home to Raleigh, Langdon's building blocks would become rocks and stones in our own attempts to recreate the "little rock village."

Joslin was born in the fall of 1970. With two children in the car, our little village became a permanent signpost for our journeys. Trips to and from the Grannies' house were measured by "How far to the little rock village?" I can't recall how many times Clauston and I said, "We *promise* to stop at the little rock village if you'll just not cry!" (or argue or will share the red crayon, or whatever). One Sunday I particularly remember, Joli dozed off and slept until we were a few miles beyond the little village. Her first waking words were, "How far to the little rock village?" When she was told we had just passed it, her two-year-old's tears were uncontrollable. We never let that happen again.

As the children changed, so did the little village. And so did Route 86. Langdon and Joslin graduated from building blocks to Lego blocks. Mr. Warren, whom we never met, but whose handiwork we always admired, added more houses and pathways built with the rocks he gathered in the fields and close-by quarry. And someone in some state road department office decided to take some of the curves and bends out of Route 86.

Soon our trips were slowed down by

construction workers, rock crushers, and heavy pavers. Though the children loved watching the big yellow trucks and machines come to life as if from the pages of their books, the day we came upon them threateningly lined up in front of the little rock village gave us pause.

Of course no harm came to our little village (I'm sure every family that ever passed by fondly calls it "*our* little village"), yet these days you must make a point to slow down, turn off the highway, and travel a few yards on the old pavement to see it well. But you can leave your car more safely now, and as Satira Warren, Henry's widow, told me, she doesn't have to worry as much about the cars and trucks whizzing by when she's mowing the grass around the make-believe town where woodland spirits must surely frolic at night.

People still stop, too. Grown men who played there when they were small boys now bring their children to see the village Henry Warren built between 1968 and 1977. "People come from all over and across the waters, even from France and Germany," Satira said. "And some

The little rock village, Shangri-La, lovingly built by Henry Warren, delights all who pass by.

people say it is a memorial to Henry Warren. Just like Washington and Lincoln have their memorials."

I awoke from my reverie when I noticed heavy thunderclouds beginning to hover overhead. The dark of the clouds foreshadowed the dark of the coming night. Even with its newly straightened stretches, Route 86 can be lonesome and unpredictable.

As I drove, faster now, my usual way, I couldn't help but muse upon my leisurely, delightful day that some people would call "wasted time." I had met new friends, relived bygone years, made new memories, and taken the time to reflect about life and the scheme of things. It

Each spring, early birds, wandering bees, and I find beauty, comfort, and nourishment in this first-to-bloom fruit tree along our most-traveled road.

was then that Robert Frost's lyrical lines came to me and I thought, no, a road does not have to be untraveled to hold romance, adventure, excitement—and to make a difference in your life.

Driving along I promised myself that another day I would follow the sign nailed to the scaly barked sycamore tree that says "Jeanette's Flowers" and points the way up a winding road that disappears over the mound. And yes, I *will* stop at the house where an angel stands in the front yard kept safe by a simple white wire fence.

The rain had begun pouring down in full force. At the exact moment that I rounded the next bend, of which there are so many on Route 86, a front porch light came on. As if by magic, that moment triggered a long-ago forgotten memory of a trip my mother and I had made along that so-familiar stretch of road many years ago on another rainy night. I could see the old Studebaker windshield wipers sweeping away the heavy raindrops that very moment.

"See the lights coming on?" she pointed out to me in her soft Southern accent. "Always remember, in every house, along every road and street in America, there is a story to be told."

"To own a bit of ground, to scratch it with a hoe, to plant seeds, and watch the renewal of life—this is the commonest delight of the race, the most satisfactory thing a man can do."

Charles Dudley Warner,
My Summer in a Garden

REFLECTIONS

"The world is a looking glass, and gives back to every man the reflection of his own face."

William Makepeace Thackeray

*L*ate in the midsummer afternoon, clouds darkened what had been a typical brilliant Southern California sky over Pasadena. My own sunny spirit faded with the sunlight as I fretted over losing the exquisite play of light and shadow on the gently rolling Gamble House garden I was visiting that day.

No more pictures today, I thought. Oh well, it's time to head back to Los Angeles anyway, I rationalized, trying to reconcile myself to something I could do nothing about. Still, I had been caught unprepared by the rather somber mood of the overcast skies that appeared without warning. Even hazy-bright would have been better than this grayness. In my disappointment, I plopped down beside a wading pool to "regroup." Suddenly, as swiftly and as quietly as it had disappeared, the sun broke through the clouds, more brilliant and vivid than before.

With the renewed sunlight burst forth a glorious scene. The graceful leaves of the waterlilies sparkled as if diamonds had been lovingly dropped down from the sky. Streams of silver sunbeams shone through the vine-covered portals of a stone wall. The still waters became as clear as a highly polished looking glass, as luminous as the prisms on a crystal chandelier. The light of the heavens was momentarily caught on earth. The spectacle was as breathtaking as a dazzling sunset. The sight was as moving as the quietly dawning sun against an azure sky.

I was spellbound. My spirit soared. My whole being was momentarily caught up in the grace and beauty of the silent light. The scene was forever etched into my mind.

In silence and full of wonder I drank it all in. Then, like before, without so much as a hint, the clouds swallowed up the sunlight and cast their dim shadows on the earth below, where, only second before, silver and gold had shone. The glorious moment had passed, but its beauty remained in my heart.

I smiled as I thought back on the day that was now ending. What did it matter if there had been a setback in my plans and my schedule? It had all worked itself out much better than I ever could have planned it. Driving back to Los Angeles, I didn't dwell on the lost time. I anticipated the quiet night ahead and the new adventures that would come tomorrow.

"To him who in the love of Nature holds
Communion with her visible forms, she speaks
A various language; for his gayer hours
She has a voice of gladness and a smile
And eloquence of beauty, and she glides
Into his darker musings, with a mild
And healing sympathy, that steals away
Their sharpness, ere he is aware."

William Cullen Bryant

COMING HOME
TO MY GARDEN

*"Though nothing can bring back the hour
Of splendour in the grass, of glory
    in the flower:
We will grieve not, rather find
Strength in what remains behind."*

William Wordsworth

I was so glad to finally be home on May Day last year. I had been away for ten days. Travels had taken me from Phoenix to Chicago to Fort Smith, Arkansas, to Washington, D. C., and finally to Baltimore before I reached Raleigh. Though I couldn't spend the entire day in the garden, late in the day I did steal a few hours there. I'll gather a May Day bouquet for myself as a little reward, I mused, leisurely strolling across the brick patio toward my waiting flowers.

Well, what were intended to be a few quiet minutes to pluck a handful of cheerful flowers turned into two stolen hours and a major weeding job that went on until the fading sun, and my own maturing eyes, made it fruitless to attempt to do more. It took only a quick glance around the border that hadn't cared one bit where I had been for the past ten days to know I had to seize the moment. After a quick run into the house I emerged in proper gardening clothes with a giant, heavy-duty garbage bag in hand.

I worked furiously. Precious pansies were in dire need of pinching back. If their almost-human, always smiling faces were going to be around in June they needed attention now!

Spent brown irises marred the beauty of those magnificent deep purple, bearded blossoms just beginning to fan out. How could they be enjoyed tomorrow if they were choked by yesterday's splendor?

I had just snipped off the last one when I saw a thousand, or so it seemed, four o'clock seedlings popping up beneath the rose bushes. They would have to be transplanted, but that was too big a job for the present. Only a few feet away, unruly mint plants were crawling among the tender variegated thyme. The thyme was struggling to survive and hardly needed any extra hindrances. It would take only a few moments to thin out the mint.

By now my once mocha-rose–polished fingernails were earth brown and chipped. My legs tingled where tiny rose thorns had, without my knowing it, pricked them minutes earlier. My back—well, a good hot bubble bath would take care of that. Still, I hadn't gathered a single flower for my May Day bouquet—the reason I had wandered into my garden to begin with. But the garbage bag was full. I could tell how much I had accomplished.

With a free spirit and guiltless conscience I turned my attention to the flowers that were blooming despite my neglect of the last few days—feathery lavender anemone, long-petaled crimson Gerber daisies, the exquisitely elegant first Cecile Brunner antique ivory roses, a single Japanese lemon-yellow

iris, and the last spray of pink bleeding heart, already fading in the toasty warm Southern sun.

I moved along the border picking from here and there, admiring the growing garden in my hand and seeing the arrangement I wanted to make in my mind's eye . . . yellow tulips and a little white candytuft.

In the blue twilight I rushed to the patch of tulips and stand of candytuft. Not one golden goblet-shaped tulip was left. Only bare curving stems and low-growing leaves remained. Two or three spindly candytuft spikes still had a top layer of white petals. All the

other stalks had begun turning to seedpods. I had completely missed their blooms this year.

Of course the blossoms I had just picked were beautiful. No one else would miss the tulips and candytuft. Yet I wondered, what else had bloomed while I was away on that trip and others?

A few late cowslip blossoms were still around and a clump of lily-of-the-valley was sending up one last stumpy spray of ruffled bells. But my bright purple, magenta, and yellow primroses had withered away without my ever seeing them. Only their crepelike deep green leaves remained. With a deep sigh I recalled a poem from my senior year in high school,

From gardens throughout the world we gather pleasures to nurture our souls and brighten our days.

Gather ye rosebuds while ye may,
Old Time is still a-flying,
And this same flower that smiles today
Tomorrow will be dying.

How Granville Smith, our English teacher, struggled to explain Robert Herrick's lines from the 1600s, when life was short. How diligently he tried to tell our worldly-wise class that those poignant feelings would have meaning to us later. We shrugged. He was right.

Tender buds. . . full-blown blossoms. How clearly nature's little flowers speak to us of fleeting time.

Those lines mean so much to me now. Yes, today life is much longer, but it is also much more complex and demanding. How we need to heed the many lessons nature has taught us through the years—lessons we have cast aside.

I stood and reflected. My blossoms had not waited for me. Neither, I sighed, do children or wives or husbands or sweethearts or parents or friends. The garden and its flowers are such a true mirror image of today's life.

In our gardens we plant young plants

and tender seeds in anticipation of watching them grow, of seeing them in their full glory, of enjoying them to their fullest. But time and circumstances—some of our own making, others beyond our control—call us away and we cannot always enjoy the gifts of our handiwork. Then, when we do have a quiet moment, how often even those are taken from us. Possessed by feelings of guilt or duty, we rush off to do jobs we feel we *must* do!

Caught up in my thoughts, I plopped down in the midst of the garden, my hands stained with the color and the scent of the mint and the thyme and the dark brown earth. To fully enjoy the flowers in our garden we must set aside a time for each blossom—but who among us can do that. Yet these days how often it is said, "You can have it all!"

I looked around me. There were tender buds, scrumptious blooms, and fading blossoms. How much more clearly nature's little flowers speak to us of life's truths than do our ambitious words. A year in the garden says so much.

My Christmas rose is beautiful in December. Perky snowdrops cheer our hearts in late January. By February and March, winter's red berries begin losing their brightness and fade—replaced by spring's early yellow buds. Through April, May, June, and July a virtual parade of flowers bloom and fade—jonquils, irises, daisies, lilies, dahlias, and, of course, the velvet-petaled roses with their prickly thorns. On sweltering hot August days, feathery ageratum blossoms

reflect the cool blue color of the sky. Sometime in late September nature sends her spectacle of fall colors to delight and tease us until November when once again we see the trees in their most beautiful laid-bare shapes and forms.

Which would we give up? None, of course.

Have it all? We do have it all. But we do not, and cannot, have it all at one time.

And so I resolved not to regret that I had missed the tulips and only glimpsed the last straggly candytuft blossoms. But I also resolved to remember: if I truly do want to catch the roses that will open next week and the dahlias that will bloom in July—if I am going to take the time to plant and nurture the chrysanthemums, to pinch the buds off every few weeks until the Fourth of July so they will open in October—then I must make the time to be in my garden when they bloom.

No, blossoms do not wait. And neither do other important things in life.

"When poppies in the garden bleed,
And coreopsis goes to seed,
And pansies, blossoming past their prime,
Grow small and smaller all the time,
When on the mown field, shrunk and dry,
Brown dock and purple thistle lie,
And smoke from forest fires at noon
Can make the sun appear the moon,
When apple seeds, all white before,
Begin to darken in the core,
I know that summer, scarcely here,
Is gone until another year."
"The End of Summer,"
Edna St. Vincent Millay

DIRECTORY

GARDEN DIRECTORY

It seems trite to say that there are beautiful gardens everywhere, but there are. If you are a garden aficionado you will want to purchase the book, *Gardens of North America and Hawaii: A Traveler's Guide* by Irene and Walter Jacob (Timber Press). Here are just a few of the many gardens I visited while writing *Pleasures of the Garden*.

Alabama

Ave Maria Grotto
St. Bernard Abbey
Cullman, AL 35055

California

The Barnyard
Highway 1 & Carmel Valley Rd.
Carmel, CA 93923

Huntington Botanical Gardens
1151 Oxford Road
San Marino, CA 91108

Robinson Jeffers Tor House
Stewart Way
Carmel, CA 93923

Delaware

Hagley Museum
Route 100 at Route 141
Wilmington, DE 19807

Rockwood Museum
610 Shipley Road
Wilmington, DE 19809

Winterthur Museum and Gardens
Henry F. du Pont Winterthur
  Museum
Winterthur, DE 19735

Florida

Busch Gardens
Route 580, off I-75
Tampa, FL 33637

Georgia

Callaway Gardens
Pine Mountain, GA 31822

Georgia's Stone Mountain Park
Stone Mountain, GA 30086

Juliet Gordon Lowe Birthplace
142 Bull Street
Savannah, GA 31401

Kentucky

Flag Fork Herb Farm
260 Flag Fork Road
Frankfort, KY 40601

Louisiana

Longue Vue
7 Bamboo Road
New Orleans, LA 70124-1065

Maryland

Ladew Topiary Garden
3535 Jarrettsville Pike
Monkton, MD 21111

Massachusetts

Habitat Institute for the Environment
10 Juniper Road
Belmont, MA 02178-0136

New York

Appledore Island
Celia Thaxter's Garden
(For information contact
The Shoals Marine Laboratory
G14 Stimson Hall
Cornell University
Ithaca, NY 14853)

North Carolina

Biltmore House & Gardens
1 North Pack Square
Asheville, NC 28801

Elizabethan Gardens
Manteo, NC 27954

Mordecai Square Historic Society
1 Mimosa Street
Raleigh, NC 27604

North Carolina State University
Arboretum
Beryl Road
Raleigh, NC 27607

Orton Plantation
Route 133
Winnabow, NC 28479

Reynolda Gardens
105 Reynolda Village
Winston-Salem, NC 27106

The Sarah P. Duke Gardens
Duke Univerrsity
Durham, NC 27706

Tryon Palace Gardens
George & Pollock Streets
New Bern, NC 28563

Ohio

Stan Hywet Hall & Gardens
14 North Portage Path
Akron, OH 44303-1399

Pennsylvania

Longwood Gardens
Route 1
Kennett Square, PA 19348

Phipps Conservatory
Schenley Park
Pittsburgh, PA 15213

South Carolina

Hopeland Gardens & Rye Patch
Whiskey Road
Aiken, SC 29801

Wayside Gardens
Route 254 North
Hodges, SC 29653

Tennessee

Blount Mansion Garden
200 W. Hill Avenue
Knoxville, TN 37901

Virginia

André Viette Farm & Nursery
Route 1, Box 16
Fishersville, VA 22939

Bacon's Castle
Route 10
Surry County, VA 23883

Colonial Williamsburg
Williamsburg, VA 32187

Monticello
Route 53
Charlottesville, VA 22906

Mount Vernon Gardens
Mount Vernon, VA 22121

Prestwould
Clarksville, VA 23927

Woodrow Wilson Birthplace
Coalter & Fredericks Streets
Stanton, VA 24401

Washington

Bloedel Reserve
7571 Northeast Dolphin Drive
Bainbridge Island, WA 98110

Washington, D.C.

Dumbarton Oaks
1703 32nd St., N.W.
Washington, D.C. 20007

Old Stone House
3051 M St., N.W.
Washington, D.C. 20007

Tudor Place
1605 32nd St., N.W.
Washington, D.C. 20007

GARDEN ITEMS

~

Every town seems to have a specialty garden shop these days, and my mailbox overflows with garden catalogues every season of the year. But there are times when a store isn't convenient and you can't find those catalogues. So here is a small listing of garden specialty shops and locations you can always turn to.

André Viette Farm & Nursery
Route 1, Box 16
Fishersville, VA 22939
Write for a catalogue that features Viette's unique perennials. For a sample of the plants available, see page 78

Cameron Park Botanicals
Highway 64 East
Raleigh, NC 27610
For a newsletter and catalogue, wonderful herbs, plants, and my favorite blue-eye tea given on page 132

Emerald Farms
409 Emerald Farm Road
Greenwood, SC 29646
Wonderful natural soaps, dried flowers, and herbs

Everyday Gardener
2947-A Old Canton Road
Jackson, MS 39216
Beautiful and helpful garden ornaments and supplies like those at right

Festival Flags
322 West Broad Street
Richmond, Virginia 23220
Joyful, festive flags that add color to your home and garden year-round, like those shown on page 156, are featured in a catalogue

Flag Fork Herb Farm
260 Flag Fork Road
Frankfort, KY 40601
Their catagloue features an ever-growing selection of herb-related items including decorations

Plants by Grant
8109 Ebenezer Church Road
Raleigh, NC 27612
Lovely, versatile, and affordable topiaries and bonsai like those at right

Signe's Little Houses
651 Millcross Road
Lancaster, PA 17601
Nellie Ahl creates custom-made playhouses for children, young and old, like the one on page 122

The Elegant Earth
1907 Cahaba Road
Birmingham, AL 35223
The figure on page 161 is one the many beautiful imported garden sculptures carried by The Elegant Earth. Catalogue available

Wayside Gardens
Route 254 North
Hodges, SC 29653
Write for their lavish catalogue featuring seeds, plants, shrubs, roses, and bulbs—everything for the garden in your mind and in your yard

Whimsical Twigs
P.O. Box 44344
Tacoma, WA 98444
Debbie and Mike Schramer create truly whimsical, elfin garden and indoor decorations like the little chair on page 123. Catalogue available

ACKNOWLEDGMENTS

I cannot imagine a more wonderful project than writing a book about gardens. Suddenly I had a legitimate reason for wandering among gentle flowers, lost in reverie, and I even had a built-in introduction to some of the nicest people I've ever met—the other people in those gardens. Yes, people who love gardens and who garden do see things differently. So thank you, each and every one whom I name here, as well as the many others with whom I chatted; those who shared their time, ideas, pleasantries, and special pleasures from the garden with me to share, in turn, with others. I wish I could send each of you a bouquet of iris, zinnias, and white periwinkle—a message, in the language of flowers, to say I think of my absent friends, with pleasure.

Sandra Ladendorf; Barbara Thomas; Pat Bender; Jocelyn Horder; Jerry Anderson; John van der Meerendork at the Bloedel Reserve; Ron and Lani Riches and Doris Ann Benoist at Monmouth; Paulette Watson and Brenda Sloan at Mary Washington College; Fran Riepe at Ladew Topiary Garden; Ann Apgar; Katie Meyer at the Century Plaza, Los Angeles; Hans Bruland at the ANA Hotel, Washington, D.C.; Catherine Babcock at the Huntington Botanical Gardens; Ted Bosley at the Gamble House; Joyce Reagin at Wayside Gardens; Bill and Suzie Holloway; Cathy Zahn at Emerald Farms; W. H. and Mildred Howell; Vivian G. Milner; Don Smith at Dumbarton Oaks; Osborne Mackie and Scott Woodbury at Tudor Place; George Husaker at the Old Stone House; Dean Norton at the Mount Vernon Gardens; Lucy Vogel; Sandy McGregor; Paul and Mary Gaston; Lou Jordan; André Viette at the André Viette Farm and Nursery; Libby Fosso, Peter Hatch, and Lynn Richmond at Monticello; Pat Hobbs at the Woodrow Wilson Birthplace; Mae Waldrup and Dixie Waldrup at The Barnyard; Karol Schmiegel and Denise Magnani at the Winterthur Museum and Gardens; Nancy Evans; Hadley Osborn and Connie Weissmuller at the Robinson Jeffers Tor House Foundation; Rebecca Hammell, Thomas Genzel, and Jack Braunlein at the Rockwood Museum; Laurie Chopin and Colvin Randall at Longwood Gardens; Mary Hirt and Philip Correll at the Hagley Museum; Julian D. Hudson at Prestwould; Mark Krisco at the Chicago Art Institute; Kent Whitworth at the Blount Mansion Garden; Brian MacFarland at Gertrude Jekyll's Glebe House; Gary Baronowski at the Phipps Conservatory; Mike and Carrie Creech at Flag Fork Herb Farm; Libby Oliver and Patrick Saylor at Colonial Williamsburg; Kelly Kleinschmidt and Margaret Tramontine at Stan Hywet Hall and Gardens; Jean Carr and William Culberson at The Sarah P. Duke Gardens, Duke University; Lydia Schmalz at Longue Vue; Jennifer Goldsborough at The Maryland Historical Society; Stephen Bohlin-Davis at the Juliet Gordon Lowe Birthplace; Alice Horton; Barbara Kirby; Dan Brooks; Ann Fox; Jane Comer; Martha McIntosh.

Special friends: Carolyn Grant; Caroline Carlton; the library staff at Saint Mary's College; Olie Adams; Ray Traylor; Harvey Bumgardener; Jane Collins; Marjie Cheshire; Gay and Cabell Birdsong; Louise Talley; Pickett Guthrie; Ginny Stevens; Lisa Vaughan; Martha Stoops; Lynn McCarthy; Lindsay and Mac Newsom; Rosemarie George; Scottie Bowers; Lucy Menius; Elizabeth Gephart; Stephen Boyd and Carol Herner; Art and Helen White; Rosemary York; Sally Clark; Catherine Hamrick.

And a full, overflowing bouquet must be sent to these people who do make work and life a pleasure, even beyond the garden: Sharon Squibb; Ken Sansone; Etya Pinker; Linda Gelbard; Michelle Sidrane; Betty A. Prashker; Pam Shepard; Gail Shanks; Chesie Hortenstine; Chip Gibson; Hazel Buchanan; Larry Sherwood; Chip Henderson; Claire Whitcomb; Janella Smyth; Carlton Long; my parents and children; and most of all to Susan Urstadt.

CREDITS

PHOTO CREDITS

Chip Henderson: pages 5, 13, 15, 16, 17, 18, 21, 24, 26, 29, 30, 34, 35, 36, 37, 38, 39, 41, 42, 44, 46, 47, 49, 50, 52, 53, 54, 55, 58, 59, 61, 62, 63, 64, 65, 68, 69, 72, 73, 74, 75, 77, 80, 83, 84, 85, 89, 91, 92, 93, 100, 101, 105, 112, 115, 117, 119, 120, 121, 122, 125, 126, 130, 131, 132, 134, 135, 138, 139, 140, 141, 144, 145, 146, 147, 150, 156, 157, 165, 166, 167, 177, 179, 183, 186.

Emyl Jenkins: pages 1, 2, 6, 7, 10, 11, 12, 13, 14, 15, 16, 20, 22, 23, 25, 27, 28, 29, 32, 33, 37, 39, 40, 44, 45, 48, 51, 52, 56, 60, 61, 66, 69, 70, 85, 86, 87, 88, 90, 96, 97, 98, 102, 103, 104, 107, 108, 109, 110, 111, 114, 116, 118, 123, 124, 128, 129, 133, 134, 136, 140, 142, 143, 148, 149, 152, 153, 154, 155, 156, 157, 158, 159, 160, 162, 163; 164, 165, 168, 170, 171, 172, 173, 174, 175, 176, 178, 180, 181, 182, 184, 185, 186, 187.

Others: Flag Farm Herbs, p. 79; Mary Washington College Special Collections, p. 130; Seny Norasinghi, pp. 131, 133; Plants by Grant, p. 13; Debbie and Mike Schramer, p. 123; Anthony Snyder, pp. 94, 99, 159; Walter Smalling, p. 53; The Elegant Earth, p. 161.

The endpapers are adapted from a fabric at Longue Vue Gardens, New Orleans, Louisiana.

ADDITIONAL CREDITS

In addition to the credits given in the captions, these credits are gratefully acknowledged:

Bloedel Reserve, p.184; Harvey Bumgardener, pp. 85, 148; Colonial Williamsburg, pp. 11, 32, 55; Jane Comer, p. 33; Dumbarton Oaks, p. 162; Dunleith, p. 162; Nancy Evans, pp. 27, 48; Paul and Mary Gaston, pp. 83, 84; Glebe House, p. 44; Hagley Museum, p. 55; Jenny Herbert, p. 159; Alice Horton, p. 122; Mildred and W. H. Howell, p. 69; Betty Hunt, p. 86; Huntington Gardens, pp. 153, 154, 155, 176, 186; Ladew Topiary Gardens, pp. 153, 158, 160, 162, 170, 172; Longue Vue Gardens, p. 16; Longwood Gardens, pp. 116, 187; Sandy McGregor, pp. 16, 47, 52, 183; Meredith College, p. 134; Monmouth Plantation, pp. 12, 164, 165; Monticello Gardens, pp. 53, 54, 125; Mordecai House, pp. 10, 45, 51, 87; Lindsay and Mac Newsom, pp. 123, 158, 159; Orton Plantation, pp. 17, 112, 150; Rockwood, p. 117; Saint Mary's College, pp. 18, 21, 77, 126, 129, 134, 149; Karol Schmiegel, pp. 27, 48, 157; Louise Talley, p. 91; Bob Timberlake, pp. 94, 99, 159; Tudor Place, pp. 1, 28; André Viette Garden, pp. 80, 122; Henry Francis du Pont Winterthur Gardens, pp. 13, 85, 117, 157, 165, 166, 179, 186; Woodrow Wilson Birthplace Gardens, p. 84.

INDEX